Catholic Youth Ministry

Saint Mary's Press wishes to thank the National Federation for Catholic Youth Ministry, particularly Bob McCarty and Kathy Carver, for their assistance, support, and enthusiasm for this project, and for their ongoing commitment to Catholic youth ministry throughout the country.

Catholic Youth Ministry: The Essential Documents is a must-have resource for youth ministers. It provides a compelling reason to develop youth ministry and keep it growing within the framework of our Catholic Tradition. This resource provides a why for what we do and moves us well beyond youth ministry that is driven by the personal wants and preferences of individual leaders. *Catholic Youth Ministry: The Essential Documents* stands as the reference resource that should be available to all youth ministry leaders.
—Greg Dobie Moser, executive director of youth and young adult ministry,
Diocese of Cleveland, and former NFCYM board member and chairperson

Catholic Youth Ministry

The Essential Documents

Laurie Delgatto, general editor

With a foreword by Robert J. McCarty

saint mary's press

The publishing team included Lorraine Kilmartin, reviewer; Mary M. Bambenek, development administrator; Mary Koehler, permissions editor; Brooke E. Saron, copy editor; Barbara Bartelson, typesetter; Andy Palmer, designer; manufacturing coordinated by the production services department of Saint Mary's Press.

Printed in the United States of America

3399

ISBN 978-0-88489-860-3

Contents

Foreword

The underlying strength of Catholic youth ministry is our common, articulated vision, promulgated by the bishops. Many other countries with organized Catholic youth ministry at the national level and denominations with a commitment to youth ministry suffer from the lack of a formally stated and shared vision of ministry with young people. The importance of an agreed-upon vision should not be underestimated or underappreciated. It has allowed the field of Catholic youth ministry to develop comprehensive approaches, models, and programs, reflecting that shared vision. That is why *Catholic Youth Ministry: The Essential Documents* is such a valuable resource.

The strategy for developing a common vision was significant in itself. The consultation process begun by the United States Catholic Conference for the original *A Vision of Youth Ministry* in 1976 and by the revamped United States Conference of Catholic Bishops for *Renewing the Vision: A Framework for Catholic Youth Ministry* in 1997 included extensive dialogue with veterans in the field of youth ministry and built upon the experiences of practitioners. This process was also used by the National Federation for Catholic Youth Ministry (NFCYM) for its series of foundational documents on particular aspects of youth ministry, which are included in this sourcebook. The NFCYM is a network of the diocesan offices of youth ministry and collaborating organizations that provides leadership, conferences, resources, and programs for enhancing Catholic youth ministry at every level of the Church. The NFCYM's commitment to significantly involving the field of youth ministry in developing foundational documents has resulted in an enduring vision with wide ownership.

A common vision provides a shared language for talking about, planning for, and implementing youth ministry. And this vision is applicable to diverse geographic settings, such as urban, suburban, and rural areas of our country, in our various cultural and ethnic communities, and in our various ministry settings, such as parishes, schools, youth movements, and community programs. Furthermore, this common vision is the starting point for the development of other resources, curriculums, and training programs designed to support our ministry. This is a significant advantage for Catholic youth ministry.

The 1997 *Renewing the Vision: A Framework for Catholic Youth Ministry* is the core document. *Renewing the Vision* built upon the 1976 document *A Vision of Youth Ministry*, the initial articulation of comprehensive youth ministry. *Renewing the Vision* further expanded the 1976 document, based on our experience of youth ministry, young people, and the Church. Once released, *Renewing the Vision* was first introduced to the field through a series of training workshops hosted by various dioceses and ministry formation providers.

The other supporting documents include *The Challenge of Adolescent Catechesis: Maturing in Faith* (1986), *The Challenge of Catholic Youth Evangelization: Called to Be Witnesses and Storytellers* (1993), and *From Age to Age: The Challenge of Worship with Adolescents* (1997). Developed and written by the NFCYM, they are anchored in the original 1976 document, and each spotlights a particular component or dimension of youth ministry. These documents also were the result of an extensive consultation with experts in the field of youth ministry.

Renewing the Vision reflects and embodies the key insights and principles from these specific documents, so much so that *Renewing the Vision, A Vision of Youth Ministry,* and these additional foundational documents inform, support, and enhance one another. The documents, though, are not meant to be a compendium of practical resources for implementing programs. However, they do provide clarity of vision, which aligns our energies, motivates our action, and focuses our ministry on defined goals.

To read these documents is to know the breadth of the vision of Catholic youth ministry as developed over a period of time and based on the experience of practitioners. To take seriously this ministry to, with, by, and for the young Church, we must begin with the shared wisdom of the faith community. Knowing these documents enables the informed youth ministry leader to transform vision into reality. This sourcebook is a treasure of collected wisdom.

Robert J. McCarty, DMin
Executive Director
of the National Federation for Catholic Youth Ministry

An In-Depth Summary of *Renewing the Vision: A Framework for Catholic Youth Ministry*

Note. Permission to reprint the complete text of *Renewing the Vision* was not granted by the United States Conference of Catholic Bishops (USCCB). What follows is an in-depth summary and discussion on the key concepts and themes found in *Renewing the Vision*, adapted from the *Total Faith™ Initiative Coordinator's Manual*, by Thomas East, Ann Marie Eckert, Leif Kehrwald, Brian Singer-Towns, and Cheryl M. Tholcke (Winona, MN: Saint Mary's Press, 2004), pages 17–27. Copyright © 2004 by Saint Mary's Press. All rights reserved. Should you wish to have access to *Renewing the Vision* in its entirety, you may view it at *www.usccb.org/laity/youth/rtvcontents*, or you may purchase a copy from the USCCB by calling 800-235-8722.

Introduction

Youth, parents, parish communities, and youth ministry leaders long for vibrant youth ministry that will engage, inspire, and empower youth for discipleship and active membership in the community. The USCCB's document *Renewing the Vision* provides a vision for this kind of dynamic ministry with youth. In the vision, youth are seen as gifted, growing, and capable of being active disciples. The parish is seen as a place where youth and their families feel welcome and participate actively. Youth ministry is described in that vision primarily as the parish's relationship with its youth, rather than as a program or a collection of activities. Through that relationship the parish community shares faith with young members.

This vision of youth ministry is broad and has numerous possibilities. In considering all the possibilities, some people can become overwhelmed. The possibilities in the vision are not intended as a checklist of things that every parish is required to provide. Rather, the possibilities provide the big picture of what Catholic youth ministry can be. Parishes find themselves in that picture, and develop their ministry with youth by connecting youth to the resources, activities, and people that constitute parish and community life.

Many people describe the vision presented in *Renewing the Vision* as "comprehensive youth ministry." To be comprehensive, parishes develop a mix of strategies and gathered events. They have a regular pattern of gathering with youth, a variety of ways to connect with youth outside of events, a means to connect with and support families of adolescents, and an intentional plan for including youth throughout parish life. The mix and emphasis of those pieces will be different for each community.

Renewing the Vision does not provide a rigid program model or a prescriptive method for developing ministry. Rather, it offers a framework, a structure that has room for parishes to develop youth ministry in a variety of ways. Like the blueprints for building a home, the framework provides five important elements that guide us:

- definition
- goals
- themes
- ministry components
- ministry settings

Definition of Catholic Youth Ministry

The definition of youth ministry offered by the bishops in *Renewing the Vision* is formed by our love for and our commitment to youth: "Youth ministry is the response of the Christian community to the needs of young people and the sharing of the unique gifts of youth with the larger community" (USCCB, *A Vision of Youth Ministry,* p. 6).

The bishops remind us to see within youth the incredible potential and capacities they have, and to respond to their present and real needs. Youth ministry does not exist because youth are particularly troubled or needy; youth are growing in ways intended by our loving God. They are encountering the joys that are a natural part of adolescence. In the midst of their growing pains, youth have wonderful gifts to offer. We minister to youth because we are Church and we follow Jesus' pattern: we respond to needs and empower youth to use and share their gifts.

Three Goals of Catholic Youth Ministry

In *Renewing the Vision*, three goals serve as directions for ministry with youth.

Goal 1: "To empower young people to live as disciples of Jesus Christ in our world today" (p. 9).   We know what young people are seeking. They seek to find the adventure of their lifetime. They look for a way to contribute something important to the world. They look for a cause to belong to, a cause in which to place

their energy and life. As a faith community, we offer young people the challenge of living as a disciple of Jesus Christ. This effort includes the following:
- providing a spiritually challenging and world-shaping vision for life
- evangelizing youth, drawing young people into a personal relationship with Jesus Christ
- calling youth to discipleship
- providing opportunities for youth to join in service, ministry, and leadership
- providing catechesis for youth
- helping youth explore their vocation

Goal 2: "To draw young people to responsible participation in the life, mission, and work of the Catholic faith community" (p. 11). We know that young people strive to be part of a community. They long to belong with others. They want to feel connected to people with whom they feel safe. As a Church, we offer young people community. We help them become more connected in their own families, in our parishes, and in the wider community.

Renewing the Vision identifies four important faith communities for young people: the family, the parish, the Catholic school, and the youth-serving organization. We help youth connect to those communities through these methods:
- supporting families of youth with resources, programs, and information
- integrating youth into the life of the parish community
- supporting community life in the Catholic school
- building participation in youth-serving organizations

Goal 3: "To foster the total personal and spiritual growth of each young person" (p. 15). We know that young people are growing. This time in their life brings dramatic physical, social, intellectual, and spiritual changes. As the Body of Christ, we offer experiences and opportunities for youth to grow in positive ways, through learning their faith and by using their gifts in service to others. As a community we use our creativity and resources to respond to youth who are seeking, striving, and growing. We foster this growth through our active engagement of youth in the life of our communities in these ways:

- supporting the development of healthy, competent, caring, and faith-filled youth
- addressing their unique developmental, social, and religious needs
- promoting Catholic identity
- using the asset-building approach to address the obstacles and challenges to healthy development

Seven Themes of Comprehensive Youth Ministry

The themes of the comprehensive vision presented in *Renewing the Vision* provide a guide for ministry development that helps us use all our resources and be inclusive and responsive in our ministry efforts.

Developmentally Appropriate

Effective ministry responds to the developmental growth of young and older adolescents by using programs and strategies that are age appropriate and strategically focused to contribute to the positive development of youth.

Adolescent Development

An important part of our picture of youth includes their tremendous growth during the years of adolescence. In *Renewing the Vision,* we are called to minister to youth whose age span encompasses both younger and older adolescents. Younger adolescents are ten years old to fourteen or fifteen years old. In school, most of those youth are in grades five through nine. With the exception of infancy, no time in life compresses more physical, intellectual, social, emotional, moral, and faith development into so brief a span. Key among those changes would be rapid physical growth, the onset of puberty, the move from concrete to abstract thinking, and the growing importance of peer groups and friendships.

Older adolescents are fifteen years old to eighteen or nineteen years old. Older adolescence is an ongoing process, beginning at age fourteen or fifteen and continuing until the early twenties. This means that some of the issues and changes for older adolescents that are addressed by youth ministry continue to be addressed by young adult ministry, which covers the age span of eighteen to thirty-five. Some key changes for older adolescents include reaching adult growth and maturity, establishing a personal identity, experiencing shifting patterns of authority, and moving toward the capacity for intimacy in relationships.

Family Friendly

Effective ministry recognizes the family as an important setting for ministry and provides links between the programs of youth ministry and the family home through information sharing, inclusive programs, and resources for families of adolescents.

Intergenerational

Effective ministry utilizes the intergenerational parish community by developing shared programs that include children, youth, and adults of all ages. The intergenerational theme is also addressed by connecting youth to adults in the community, which includes adults mentoring youth, as well as linking youth as mentors with younger members of the parish.

Multicultural

Effective ministry provides for ministry to youth in the context of their culture and their ethnic heritage. Effective ministry also promotes crosscultural understanding and appreciation.

Communitywide Collaboration

Effective ministry promotes collaboration with leaders, agencies, and congregations in the wider community. This collaboration includes sharing information, sponsoring programs, and developing advocacy efforts.

Leadership

Effective ministry mobilizes the people of the faith community to become involved in youth ministry efforts by providing diverse roles and leadership commitments for adults and youth.

Leadership for Youth Ministry: It Takes a Parish

An exciting part of the vision for youth ministry is that everyone in the community can play a role. The whole community can pray for young people, make youth feel welcome, and support ministry efforts. Many organizations, adults, and youth can find a place to make youth ministry happen. It is all about focusing the gifts of the community in a common direction.

The Coordinator of Youth Ministry

Supporting youth ministry takes leadership. In many parishes, choosing a single leader or a small group of leaders was the first and only thing the community did to support youth ministry. This left too much for too few people to do. Imagine an orchestra conductor who takes the podium and uses the baton to begin the symphony. As he starts the piece, he also runs down to play each instrument, running from seat to seat, trying to be the whole orchestra. It just would not work. The conductor needs the musicians. A coordinator of youth ministry is like the conductor, because he or she tries to keep the many gifted players in sync, bringing each group of instruments into the piece at the right time. "Ministry coordinators have a central role in facilitating the people, programming, and resources of the faith community on behalf of a comprehensive ministry effort with adolescents" (*Renewing the Vision,* p. 24).

The Coordinating Team: Keeping an Eye on the Big Picture

The coordinator of youth ministry works hand in hand with a coordinating team to keep an eye on the big picture for youth ministry. This team of youth and adults organizes the various ministry efforts and helps connect the variety of strategies and programs. In this schema are many different roles for the people who are willing to help. There are many roles for people who like to speak or teach. There are many more roles for people who work behind the scenes in planning, hospitality, transportation, administration, and organization of the various ministries. The key is to match people's energy and gifts with a youth ministry strategy.

Flexible and Adaptable Programming

Effective ministry provides flexible and adaptable program structures and ministry responses to address the variety of youth and families in our communities.

Creating Many Doors for Youth to Enter

Renewing the Vision directs parishes to create "flexible and adaptable program structures [to] address the changing needs and life situations of today's young people and their families" (p. 25).

Parishes that effectively minister to youth provide a variety of ways for youth with different interests to be involved. Some youth are looking for a community they can join to be part of social, faith-formation, and service programs. Other youth seek out specific interests. For instance, some youth in our parishes are already attached to a peer group. They might be involved in band, choir, sports, or a service club. They would like to connect with the parish but do not necessarily want to join a group. Those young people might be attracted to faith-formation programs, service programs, or retreats, but they may not want to join the youth group.

Many youth in our parishes attend Catholic high schools that have strong religious education and service components. For those youth the door to youth ministry might be involvement in ministry, leadership, or service. They might be paired with an adult to learn how to become a lector or a catechist for younger children. They might help take leadership in developing ministry programs for younger adolescents. Some youth are going to begin their involvement in the parish by being part of the social and community-building components. Different starting points create doors for young people to enter into the home of our parish.

Eight Components of Comprehensive Youth Ministry

The components describe eight specific areas of the mission of the Church that work together to provide ministry with adolescents. "These components provide a framework for the Catholic community to *respond* to the needs of young people and to *involve* young people in sharing their unique gifts with the larger community" (*Renewing the Vision,* p. 26).

The components support and enhance one another. Ministry becomes more effective when the ministry response is balanced across the eight ministry areas. This balance is not necessarily achieved by developing separate ministry activities and strategies for each component; sometimes a single event, such as a retreat, incorporates several ministry components. A balanced approach to the following components, taken from *Renewing the Vision,* takes place over a season or year of ministry.

Advocacy

"The ministry of advocacy engages the Church to examine its priorities and practices to determine how well young people are integrated into the life, mission, and work of the Catholic community. It places adolescents and families first by analyzing every policy and program—domestic, parish-based, diocesan, and international—for its impact on adolescents and families. Poor, vulnerable, and at-risk adolescents have first claim on our common efforts. The ministry of advocacy struggles against economic and social forces that threaten adolescents and family life, such as poverty, unemployment, lack of access to affordable health care, lack of decent housing, and discrimination. The ministry of advocacy supports policies and programs that support and empower adolescents and their families and works to overcome poverty, provide decent jobs, and promote equal opportunity. In all advocacy efforts we must remember to focus on adolescents and families with the greatest need" (*Renewing the Vision,* p. 27). This is the "option for the poor" in action (Domestic Social Policy, International Policy, and Marriage and Family Life Committees, *Putting Children and Families First,* p. 14).

Catechesis

"The ministry of catechesis helps adolescents *develop* a deeper relationship with Jesus Christ and the Christian community, and *increase* their knowledge of the core content of the Catholic faith. The ministry of Catechesis also helps young people *enrich* and *expand* their understanding of the Scriptures and the sacred tradition and their application to life today, and *live* more faithfully as disciples of Jesus Christ in their daily lives, especially through a life of prayer, justice, and loving service. Genuine faith is a total response of the whole person—mind, heart, and will. The ministry of catechesis fosters growth in Catholic faith in all three dimensions—trusting (heart), knowing and believing (mind), and doing (will)" (p. 29).

Community Life

"The ministry of community life *builds* an environment of love, support, appreciation for diversity, and judicious acceptance that models Catholic principles; *develops* meaningful relationships; and *nurtures* Catholic faith. The content of our message will be heard only when it is lived in our relationships and community life. To teach compassion, generosity, tolerance, peace, forgiveness, acceptance, and love as gospel values and to identify ourselves as Christians requires us to live these values in our interactions with young people and in our community life. . . . The ministry of community life is not only *what* we do (activity), but *who* we are (identity) and *how* we interact (relationships)" (p. 34).

Evangelization

"The ministry of evangelization shares the good news of the reign of God and invites young people to hear about the Word Made Flesh. Drawing from Jesus' example, evangelization involves the community's pronouncement and living witness that the reign of God has become realized in and through Jesus. The starting point for the ministry of evangelization 'is our recognition of the presence of God already in young people, their experiences, their families, and their culture. . . . Evangelization, therefore, enables young people to uncover and name the experience of a God already active and present in their lives. This provides an openness to the gift of the Good News of Jesus Christ'" (*Renewing the Vision,* p. 36, quoting *The Challenge of Catholic Youth Evangelization,* pp. 7–8).

"The ministry of evangelization incorporates several essential elements: *witness, outreach, proclamation, invitation, conversion,* and *discipleship*" (*Renewing the Vision,* pp. 36–37).

Justice and Service

"The ministry of justice and service *nurtures* in young people a social consciousness and a commitment to a life of justice and service rooted in their faith in Jesus Christ, in the Scriptures, and in Catholic social teaching; *empowers* young people to work for justice by concrete efforts to address the causes of human suffering; and *infuses* the concepts of justice, peace, and human dignity into all ministry efforts" (p. 38).

Leadership Development

"The ministry of Leadership Development *calls forth, affirms,* and *empowers* the diverse gifts, talents, and abilities of adults and young people in our faith communities for comprehensive ministry with adolescents. Leadership roles in adolescent ministry are key. Leaders must be trained and encouraged. This approach involves a wide diversity of adult *and* youth leaders in a variety of roles. Many will be involved in direct ministry with adolescents, others will provide support services, and yet others will link the ministry effort to the resources of the broader community" (p. 40).

Pastoral Care

"The ministry of pastoral care is a compassionate presence in imitation of Jesus' care of people, especially those who were hurting and in need. The ministry of Pastoral Care involves *promoting* positive adolescent and family development through a variety of positive (preventive) strategies; *caring* for adolescents and families in crisis through support, counseling, and referral to appropriate community agencies; *providing guidance* as young people face life decisions and make moral choices; and *challenging* systems that are obstacles to positive development *(advocacy)*. Pastoral care is most fundamentally a relationship—a ministry of compassionate presence. This was Jesus' caring stance toward all people, especially those who were hurting or in need. Pastoral care enables healing and growth to take place within individuals and their relationships. It nurtures growth toward wholeness" (p. 42).

Prayer and Worship

"The ministry of prayer and worship *celebrates* and *deepens* young people's relationship with Jesus Christ through the bestowal of grace, communal prayer, and liturgical experiences; it *awakens* their awareness of the spirit at work in their lives; it *incorporates* young people more fully into the sacramental life of the Church, especially Eucharist; it *nurtures* the personal prayer life of young people; and it *fosters* family rituals and prayer" (p. 44).

Settings
for Comprehensive Youth Ministry

Often, as youth ministry leaders, we limit our thinking about the settings in which ministry to young people can occur. Consider the following four settings, and the possibilities open up.

Youth

Direct ministry to and with youth, using activities and strategies, is the first setting to consider. This is the setting we most commonly associate with youth ministry. It includes the variety of ways that we gather young people: youth group meetings, religious education programs, sacramental preparation, socials, sporting events, youth retreats, youth service events, and special youth prayer services. Ministry in the youth setting also includes individualized efforts and ways we connect directly with youth without gathering them, such as e-mail prayer messages or a parish ministry presence at youth football games and concerts.

Family

Ministry in the family setting includes the variety of ways that we connect with families of adolescents. This includes providing resources and programs that support parents, as well as strategic opportunities that bring the family together. In this setting we also support the ways that family members minister to and with each other in the home. For example, we can provide suggestions for family prayer or fun time for families of adolescents as they share faith together in the home. With strategies as simple as developing family information packets for youth programs, parents will know what their children are experiencing, and they will be better prepared to support their children's efforts.

Parish

The parish setting includes the many ways that youth experience ministry through the life of the parish itself. For example, how do we include the gifts of youth and respond to their needs through our parish liturgies? Some communities prepare liturgies that include youth in the liturgical ministries and are intentional about mentioning, in prayers and homilies, people and issues that matter to youth.

The parish's community life also becomes a place to minister to youth when we pay attention to their needs and gifts. When planning events such as a parish mission or a parishwide service event, consider how those events can touch the lives of young people.

In *Renewing the Vision*, parishes are called "to become 'youth-friendly' communities in which youth have a conspicuous presence" (p. 13). Those communities have the following characteristics:
- They make youth feel welcome.
- They listen to youth.
- They respond to the needs of youth.
- They support youth with prayer, time, facilities, and money.
- They see youth as resources.
- They empower the gifts of youth.
- They provide meaningful roles for youth in the community.
- They provide for intergenerational relationships.
- They connect youth to role models and mentors.
- They include youth in the life of the parish: prayer, learning, serving, and celebrating.

The Wider Community

Ministry to youth in the wider community connects youth and families to programs and resources beyond the parish. Examples are participation in interparish, interchurch, and diocesan events, and ways that we can connect youth and families to programs, resources, and events in the civic community. Connecting youth to service in hospitals, soup kitchens, and homeless shelters is a wonderful way for youth to develop their gifts. We take advantage of our shared strength when we come together with other people and agencies in the wider community as advocates for youth.

Conclusion: Putting the Framework Together

Together the definition, goals, themes, components, and settings provide the framework for developing our unique response as a parish community. This framework provides a guide for developing comprehensive youth ministry and is designed to do the following:

- utilize each of the Church's ministries—advocacy, catechesis, community life, evangelization, justice and service, leadership development, pastoral care, prayer and worship—in an integrated approach to achieving the three goals for ministry with adolescents
- provide developmentally appropriate programs and activities that promote personal and spiritual growth for young and older adolescents
- enrich family life and promote the faith growth of families of adolescents
- incorporate young people fully into all aspects of Church life and engage them in ministry and leadership in the faith community
- create partnerships among families, schools, churches, and community organizations in a common effort to promote positive youth development

(Renewing the Vision, p. 20)

A Church that responds to youth by creating comprehensive youth ministry is a place where youth and their families will find what they need to belong deeply, grow in faith, and find a way to share their gifts. Pope John Paul II describes this vision for Church:

This is what is needed: *a Church for young people,* which will know how to speak to their heart and enkindle, comfort and inspire enthusiasm in it with the joy of the Gospel and the strength of the Eucharist; a Church which will know how to invite and to welcome the person who seeks a purpose for which to commit his whole existence; a Church which is not afraid to require much, after having given much; which does not fear asking from young people the effort of a noble and authentic adventure, such as that of the following of the Gospel. (1995 World Day of Prayer for Vocations, no. 2)

Chapter 2

From Age to Age:
The Challenge of Worship with Adolescents

Introduction

Our Role

The National Federation for Catholic Youth Ministry (NFCYM) is an advocate for the needs of Catholic youth in the United States. As a federation of diocesan leaders, we collaborate with other pastoral, liturgical, and catechetical leaders to develop ministries *to, with, by, and for youth.* As advocates, we are committed to fully engaging youth in the life of the Church.

Our Concern

Prayer and worship are central to the life of the Catholic Church. Who we are as Christians and how we pray are intimately bound together. Therefore, worship is foundational to a comprehensive youth ministry. The experience of the community's worship is often the doorway by which youth enter the other dimensions of parish life. The noticeable absence or disengagement of the young generation from worship is a cause for concern, not just for youth ministers, but for the life of the Church. At worship, all the generations join in praising God and are sent to be Good News to the world. To be most effective in its mission, the Church needs all its members to be fully involved.

Our Audience

This document is one part of a multiple-year response by the NFCYM to concerns regarding youth participation in worship. We write it primarily for youth ministers and youth who exercise leadership with their peers. We have sought the advice and support of bishops, pastors, liturgists, liturgical musicians, and catechetical leaders. Our collaboration has been fruitful. We believe this document can foster a similar dialogue among youth, pastoral, catechetical, and liturgical leaders in local dioceses and parishes.

Our Focus

We are primarily speaking about adolescents between the ages of thirteen and nineteen, or those who would be in grades 6–12 in school. They are at a critical point in their spiritual, social, intellectual, and physical development. Although through the social sciences we know more now than we did even a few decades ago about adolescence, our society and culture are constantly changing, and the issues of adolescents change as well. Youth ministers and other church leaders face a unique set of challenges when responding to these changes. Through this NFCYM Youth and Worship Initiative, we want to raise awareness of current issues that affect the worship experiences of adolescents and provide strategies for parishes to develop their own pastoral plan for responding to these issues.

Our Process

Youth also need to respond to these challenges. That is why we have involved youth in the preparation of this document, and their voices are added to our text and strategies. Statements written by youth who represented their peers at a National Youth and Worship Forum in November 1995 [appear above]. We have not edited their comments substantially so we could explore the original meaning and set a context for dialogue. (Editor's note: In the original NFCYM publication, the quotes were scattered throughout the document. For formatting purposes they have simply been listed here).

Through the homily, youth need to learn about their Church community. Through understanding, they will feel as if they belong.

We are not changing tradition, only enhancing it.

Youth must not wait for the Church to surround them; youth must surround the Church.

Community is the big symbol of Church for adolescents.

Youth need to understand exactly what the sacraments are and why we receive them.

Youth catechesis for liturgy needs to be interactive. It's important to be simple and direct. It must be concise, clear, and dynamic.

Youth want to become involved in the choir/music of the liturgy.

Liturgy works best when you have visual aids; when people are involved and interested.

The presider should be personal and personable for the benefit of everyone in the parish.

It is important for youth to be personally invited to assist in the planning process.

Liturgy works best when Jesus is the center; when reverence and love is practiced by all.

Liturgy works best when the youth have a say in what is going on.

Liturgical ministries should be more readily available for all youth who have a desire to participate.

Youth should be involved in every Mass.

Our Commitment

We realize that it may not be possible to provide immediate answers or solutions for some issues these youth have raised. We consider it always essential, however, to involve youth in developing a pastoral response, and community involvement is important in the faith development of the young. We are also committed to providing and promoting additional resources that can aid this process.

Special Note

We use the term *liturgy* inclusively in this document to refer to all types of liturgical celebrations. We acknowledge, however, that for most youth "liturgy," "going to Church," and "mass" are synonymous. Most of the examples and strategies that follow refer to

Sunday Mass, though confirmation and the sacraments of healing, in particular, are also significant liturgical experiences for many teens.

Our Purpose and Aim

Gathering Everyone Around the Lord's Table

"From age to age you gather a people to yourself, so that from east to west a perfect offering may be made to the glory of your name" (Eucharistic Prayer 3, in the *Sacramentary*, p. 552). From one generation to the next it is always Christ who gathers us and is present when the Church prays and sings. Each age has a responsibility to pass on the tradition of gathering to break the bread and recall the Lord's presence. We have a responsibility to join in that celebration according to our gifts and talents. Each of us is called to be part of the community Christ leads. The experience of that community may be changing or may be different for each of us. It is the same Lord, however, who gathers all generations. "There are varieties of gifts, but the same Spirit" (1 Cor. 12:4).

Many youth are not present at our parish worship. Many others are present but feel alienated from the group. This is the source of our concern and the reason for our action. As a community, we are less complete when these teens are not with us. We as the Mystical Body of Christ are less whole. When these adolescents are not visible and their voices are not heard at the liturgy, we are less able to give thanks and glory for the good works that God accomplishes through us. Our prayer is less complete when we do not include the faith experiences of adolescents and when young people's enthusiasm is missing.

The work of liturgy is our response to Christ, because "to accomplish so great a work, Christ is always present in His Church, especially in her liturgical celebrations" (*Sacrosanctum Concilium, Constitution on the Sacred Liturgy*, no. 7). Christ invites each of us to join and participate fully in the paschal mystery by celebrating the sacraments. The grace of God available to us in the liturgy has the power to change our lives, but we must be open to the gift. As youth ministers and advocates, we want all youth to know that the

Church does not just *expect* them to attend the liturgy but, in the Spirit of Christ, *invites* them to join us in giving thanks and praise. We need their enthusiasm and adventurous spirit to make our worship more fully alive. The whole community needs to accept responsibility for the liturgy, and we invite youth to gather with us and take their rightful place in the Church's worship life.

Our aim is to encourage and support youth involvement in the Christian lifestyle, in the liturgical ministries, and in the assembly. All three are essential to a balanced pastoral plan. Such involvement is young peoples' "right and duty by reason of their baptism" (*Sacred Liturgy*, no. 14). Many youth are already actively participating and using their gifts for the good of the community's worship and their peers. They give witness that in these new generations, Christ is still proclaiming his gospel and the people are responding to God by both song and prayer. The faith experiences of adolescents enrich our own sense of the continuing presence of Christ's Spirit in the world and give us hope.

Greater youth participation in the liturgy will not occur without an *intentional* effort to seek and encourage it. Parents, pastors, parish priests, youth and youth leaders, liturgy committees, and concerned individuals need to create a local pastoral plan. Unfortunately, too many parish members are content to describe youth only as the "future church." Young people are members of the Church now. We need to *intentionally* invite them to participate in our ongoing mission. Pope John Paul II stated:

> *The Church has so much to talk about with youth, and youth have so much to share with the Church.* This mutual dialogue, by taking place with great cordiality, clarity and courage, will provide a favorable setting for the meeting and exchange between generations, and will be a source of richness and youthfulness for the Church and civil society. (*Christifideles Laici, The Vocation and the Mission of the Lay Faithful in the Church and in the World*, no. 46)

There are barriers to that dialogue and collaboration. One difficulty is young people's attitude toward the Church. Many youth ministers describe their work as similar to preaching the Gospel in another culture. Because the Gospel is so countercultural, it is often a difficult message for adolescents to hear. A primary developmental need for teens is to fit into a peer group. Consequently, there can be tremendous peer pressure against participating or taking an active role in faith experiences or in liturgical celebrations. Parents and youth ministers are sometimes unwilling to challenge this status quo, but they must challenge it.

Another difficulty is adults' distrustful attitude toward youth. Many teens who have attended leadership events describe their disappointment at not being given meaningful tasks when they return to the parish, or simply at the lack of opportunities for involvement. "The starting point for youth evangelization is our recognition of the presence of God already in young people, their experiences, their families and their culture" (NFCYM, *The Challenge of Catholic Youth Evangelization*, p. 7). We invite teens to celebrate with us liturgically Christ's presence in their lives. We must also challenge distrustful attitudes and procedures that prevent youth from significant parish involvement.

Parents, youth ministers, and pastoral leaders can invite, encourage, and guide participation, but gradually the responsibility for involvement shifts to the adolescent. Some youth choose to dissociate themselves from the family faith practices during these developmental periods of their lives, causing great turmoil in families and anguish for parents. "While we can legitimately expect participation on the part of young people, we cannot manipulate or coerce a particular faith response" (NFCYM, *The Challenge of Adolescent Catechesis*, no. 24). Parents and pastoral leaders must exercise patience when addressing youth who feel alienated from our parishes. When we extend our invitations to renewed participation, we need to respect teens' natural developmental issues and respond with appropriate persistence. This requires a delicate balance. Young people face tremendous challenges in their lives. Yet, by its nature, liturgy challenges all of us to take up the Gospel.

Promoting Renewal of the Liturgy

We call for the continuing renewal of the liturgy, not only for adolescents, but for every member of the Church. "Zeal for the promotion and restoration of the liturgy is rightly held to be a sign of the providential dispositions of God in our time, as a movement of the Holy Spirit in His Church" (*Sacred Liturgy*, no. 43). The renewal of the liturgy is a response to that Spirit and not simply change for change's sake. Adolescents assist our faith communities by calling us to the youthfulness and vitality of the Spirit. We do so by expressing ourselves at worship in ways that are appropriate to our own day and age.

The Second Vatican Council's *Constitution on the Sacred Liturgy* laid the groundwork for further renewal, trusting that the Spirit would guide future efforts. It called for careful investigation from theological, historical, and pastoral perspectives. We trust that the simplicity and tradition of our rites are not in jeopardy when we place our efforts under the guidance of that same Spirit and invite young people to join us in discerning our response.

The simple faith of youth and their candor can open us to the movement of that spirit of renewal. Adolescents' need for variety and their quick admission of boredom challenge us. Still, the nature of liturgy involves tradition and an expected amount of repetition. Youth can understand this basic dynamic of ritual. They experience and anticipate many rituals in school, social, and family settings. Young people expect and enjoy the repetition of "hit songs," popular fashions, and "blockbuster" movies. Therefore, we trust that the renewal to which youth challenge us is a change of heart—the same *metanoia* (conversion) to which Jesus invited us. We need to challenge youth to the same conversion. As young people become familiar with liturgical rituals and actively involve themselves in the celebration, the church's worship will become more vibrant.

The liturgical reforms begun at the Second Vatican Council have led to five key developments. They can be summarized as:
- A greater awareness and participation in the liturgy by the faithful;
- A diversification and fulfillment of ministries within liturgical celebrations;
- A restoration of the importance of the Word within liturgical celebrations;
- The use of the vernacular for the liturgy;
- Adaptation of the rites to the needs of our own times.

The renewal of the liturgy we advocate for adolescents and the Church is rooted in these five developments.

A Greater Awareness and Participation in the Liturgy by the Faithful

We raise a special concern for adolescents at liturgy that is similar to the Church's concern for children, knowing that circumstances in which teens grow are also "not always favorable to their spiritual progress" (Congregation for Divine Worship, *Directory for Masses with Children*, no. 1). Traditionally, the Church has only made a distinction between children and adults and has only recently specifically acknowledged adolescence. More is known today than ever before about the needs of adolescents as a specific developmental group within post-industrial societies. This knowledge of adolescence can help pastors and other ministers to invite youth to full participation in the community's worship. If the liturgy is to have its deepest effect in the lives of adolescents, then we must "show an ability to understand their roles and to accept them" (Sacred Congregation for the Clergy, *General Catechetical Directory*, no. 82).

A Diversification and Fulfillment of Ministries Within Liturgical Celebrations

We believe that when we make adolescents aware of their role in the assembly and give them greater opportunities to participate in the liturgical ministries, they will respond to the invitation. We invite young people to give their gifts as fully as they can at this stage in their lives. As communities of faith, we need to be open to youth in our midst—not just as future members but for the Spirit of Christ that they already reveal *as adolescents*. Parents, liturgical leaders, and religious educators need to affirm the talents they observe in youth and provide assistance as teens discern their response to the call of ministry.

A Restoration of the Importance of the Word Within Liturgical Celebrations

The assembly gathers for liturgy believing that God has acted in human history and, more particularly, in their own history. At the liturgy, young and old alike look for meaning in their lives through the Word, which is symbol and sign for all generations. The diversity of generations and life experiences of those present, however, makes the homilist's task difficult. Youth grow in faith and appreciation of the power of liturgy to name meaning in their lives when homilists make an intentional effort to preach the Word in a manner teens can also understand and to which they can relate. Through this effective preaching and attention to the prayers, liturgical leaders invite adolescents to greater participation in liturgy.

The Use of the Vernacular for the Liturgy

The Second Vatican Council allowed the liturgy to be translated into the "vernacular," which is more than simple translation. Vernacular implies a desire to explore how the Word is fulfilled in our hearing, complete with nuances reflecting current cultural issues and examples. Youth often describe a person who speaks their vernacular as "someone who talks at our level." Today's vernacular is complex and always changing, but the ritual language of liturgy is constant. There are natural differences and tensions between the language of our everyday lives and the language of liturgy that may be developmentally difficult for youth to hear. Adults need to assist youth in understanding and appreciating the meaning of the ritual language of liturgy and in hearing it "in the vernacular" (*Sacred Liturgy*, no. 36). In the process, youth may assist the full assembly in understanding how the Word and other dimensions of the liturgy can relate more directly to current culture.

Adaptation of the Rites to the Needs of Our Own Times

The *Constitution on the Sacred Liturgy* specified further reform by calling for the legitimate variations and adaptations to different groups, regions, and peoples, especially in mission lands (see no. 38). By their nature, the rituals and symbols of liturgy are timeless and yet always open to the Spirit's movement. The Constitution's principle of adaptation provided the vehicle by which the rites could further respond to each new generation. Today's adolescents present a challenge to liturgical ministers to prepare the symbols, prayers, music, and rituals of the liturgy in a way that invites their greater response. Most adolescents are not asking for changes in the liturgy. Rather, they look for a basic understanding of the rites so they can more fully participate in the tradition. Liturgical leaders and religious educators should explain any adaptations and variations in the rites in a nondidactic way so that all members of the assembly can join in confidently.

Accomplishing Our Purpose

We invite young people to add their faith experiences to the unbroken tradition and unchanging faith of the church as we celebrate the liturgy in our own day and age. Three foundations ground our efforts to engage youth more fully in the liturgy: our belief in the charisms of youth, the partnership of family and community, and the effect of catechesis. Each of these will be addressed more fully in the next section. These foundations also help shape the specific principles and strategies named later in this document.

Foundations for Renewal

Reclaiming the Charisms of Adolescents

By Attending to the Word

I write to you, young people,
    because you are strong
    and the word of God abides in you.

(1 John 2:14)

By their presence, youth continue to be part of God's saving plan in our own day and age. The Word of God *abides* in young people. The Word is the source of their faith and strength to do the will of God. By their baptism, young people are called to a life of faith and to take part in the sacred mysteries. They participate in ways authentic to their situation in life, exercising the charisms bestowed upon them by the Spirit.

By Adopting the Attitude of Christ

Jesus took care to single out children and youth as he reached out to the marginalized, the "haibiru" in the Old Testament. His will was to "let the little children come to me" (Mark 10:14). Children and youth were important to Jesus' preaching about the Kingdom. They had the simplicity to listen and hear his message, a meaning that was "hidden from the wise and the intelligent clever" (Matt. 11:25). The Church must seek to rekindle the very special love displayed by Christ towards the young man in the Gospel: "Jesus, looking at him, loved him" (Mark 10:21). "For this reason the church does not tire of proclaiming Jesus Christ to young people" (*The Vocation and the Mission of the Lay Faithful,* no. 47). We must adopt this attitude of Christ—reaching out in love and inviting youth to come to him.

By Remaining Youthful in Spirit

"The Church looks to the young; or rather, the Church in a special way sees herself in the young" (*Dilecti Amici*, no. 15). Just as youth are adolescents coming to maturity, so they call the Church to be a people growing into the full stature of Christ. Those who are called to worship, especially to the table of the Eucharist, are invited to understand themselves as a people who are "on the way," a "pilgrim people" who are celebrating "what is" in the firm hope of "what is yet to be." Youth, then, challenge the rest of the Church not to become settled and sedentary, never to experience itself as fully established or absolutely complete. Youth—in their vitality, their questioning and exploration, their stretching, their transition from childhood to adulthood, their need for dependence in the middle of searching for independence—in all of these things, youth mirror for us the face of a church with a youthful heart. Youth engage us in a sense of wonder and awe about the present that evokes a joy and hopefulness for the future.

By Accepting Youth as They Are

The Church has much to gain from reclaiming the *charism of adolescence* that youth represent. It must also be prepared to accept the fullness of their situation in life. Adolescents are neither "grownup children" nor "little adults." Both those images prevent us from valuing youth as people with gifts for the Church now. Teens are more than just people "in transition." Their changeable attitudes, however, are sometimes difficult to understand. The normal development of adolescents can also be a source of tension in parishes and families. It can also be a unique opportunity for the Christian community to affirm, support, and challenge young people to grow as people and believers.

By Developing Youth Charisms

In addition to the *charism of adolescence,* youth possess a variety of particular charisms that benefit the Church. Although these and other personal qualities are not exclusive to adolescents, the following five seem particularly evident in young people. The Scriptures provide some images of these charisms in action.

The Charism of Vision. The disciples gave witness on the day of Pentecost that the Spirit rests upon "all flesh" (Acts 2:17), that is, all people. Their reference was to the prophet Joel and their testimony gives us a link between the Old and New Testaments.

> Then afterward
>> I will pour out my spirit on all flesh;
> your sons and your daughters shall prophesy,
>> your old men shall dream dreams,
>> and your young men shall see visions.
> Even on the male and female slaves,
>> in those days, I will pour out my spirit.
>
> (Joel 2:28–29)

The visions of today's adolescents offer us opportunities to ask "what if" questions about our common life. What if we really lived our worship? The visions of the young challenge us to grow as witnesses of Christ's saving action in our lives.

The Charism of Questioning. In the Jewish tradition, the questions of the young were ritualized (see Exod. 12:26). At the Seder, they did not hear these questions as a challenge to the tradition. Rather, the questions were opportunities for the community to retell the story of God's saving acts and a way for young and old alike to reenter the ritual moment. Today's adolescents present our parishes with a similar opportunity to retell the story and celebrate the meaning of the liturgy—the paschal mystery.

The Charism of Service. Mary, the model of Christian service, was a young woman when she was asked to become the mother of Christ (see Luke 1:26–38). Her unquestioning "yes" is an example to us all. Today's adolescents are eager to serve and do so in many different settings within and outside parishes. Their charity, compassion, and caring are simple and direct. Their lives are less complicated by personal needs or agenda than adults'. Their idealism and generosity renew our mission to serve as church.

The Charism of Enthusiasm. The parable of the five wise and five foolish young women (see Matt. 25:1–13) provides a contrasting image of both loyal enthusiasm as well as "live for the moment" attitudes among the young. Youth are risk-takers and their energy can be contagious. Sometimes they cannot see the consequences of the risks they take. When they succeed, however, their joy is intense. Their first professions of personal belief are deeply moving to those privileged to hear them on retreats, during service experiences, and in other catechetical settings. Their enthusiasm supports our taking risks as a community to spread the Gospel.

The Charism of Prophecy. The call of the prophet Jeremiah (see Jer. 1:4–10) is often used in prayer services and liturgies with adolescents. Jeremiah, a young man at first fearful to speak God's word, is presented as model and challenge to youth to let their voices for truth be heard within the community. Through their honesty and candor, adolescents call us to accountability. Today's adolescents prophesy with their very lives. The danger they face in their struggle to grow up healthy and whole in our culture of violence is a message for our communities to heed.

Adolescents want to give their gifts. We give thanks to God for the charisms of youth in our midst. We need to make it easier for them to give, particularly in the liturgical ministries. As Pope John Paul II stated:

> This church today, in the United States and in all the other countries from which you come, needs the affection and cooperation of her young people, the hope of her future. In the church each one has a role to play and all together we build up the one body of Christ, the one people of God. ("World Youth Day Prayer Vigil," in *Origins*, August 26, 1993, p. 185)

Encouraging the Partnership of Youth, Family, and Community

By Challenging Stereotypes

Contrary to some popular stereotypes, youth still want a close connection with community and family. Teens' need for family and parental approval, however, is always in dynamic tension with their need for acceptance by and inclusion in a peer group. They also intertwine their choice of friends with their search for personal identity. This is particularly true for younger adolescents.

By Following the Example of Jesus

The scriptural passage depicting Jesus in discourse with the elders at the temple (Luke 2:41–52) gives us an image of the interrelationship between community and family in the faith lives of youth. From a developmental viewpoint, the story is an example of healthy adolescent growth. From a catechetical viewpoint, the passage shows a model of how family and parish need to support and guide youth in a critical stage of their lives. From a liturgical viewpoint, the scene gives us an example of how youth surprise us with their gifts and challenges, and their desire to take their rightful place in our rituals.

Consider for the moment that this is a story of a typical adolescent today. Jesus, as a twelve-year-old, is searching for personal meaning and identity. He listens to the elders in the temple, asks questions, and provides his own viewpoints. He proclaims the Scriptures and then his purpose—to be *in my Father's house.* He is aware of his mission and calling—his charism. Developmentally, Jesus is doing what all adolescents need to do by following his parents on the journey, yet choosing to make his own way. At the same time, Jesus' parents are somewhat unaware of the shift, assuming that he is *in the group of travelers* as any normal *child* would be. When they notice his absence and return to Jerusalem, they encounter the *adolescent* Jesus interacting with the community in a different way than they expected. Their response is worry and wonder—normal reactions for parents of adolescents. Joseph and Mary respond appropriately by challenging Jesus to account for his actions and by expressing their feelings of concern. Jesus, the *adolescent,* responds—with *vision, question, enthusiasm, prophecy, and a spirit of service*—that he was only doing what he was supposed to do.

By Fulfilling Necessary Roles

This scene in the story has some important developmental, catechetical, and liturgical dynamics worth exploring. Jesus, the adolescent, needs to hear the concern and love of his parents as he explores his new personal awareness and faith questions. Jesus needs to know of their support even as he makes their lives difficult. At the same time, he needs the community to provide a welcoming, supportive place for him to ask those questions, develop those skills, and become aware of the traditions and rituals. The balance of the person, family, and community, all exercising their natural roles, is essential to healthy development and catechesis. The balance of roles supports Jesus as he returns to Nazareth with his parents to *advance in wisdom, age, and grace.*

By Working Together

We suggest that the same balance of roles is just as essential for liturgy to become a vibrant experience for today's adolescents. The *Directory for Masses with Children* states that when introducing children to the liturgy, "All who have a part in the formation of children should consult and work together toward one objective" (no. 9). The goal is to assist children in participating in the liturgy in a way appropriate to their developmental abilities and tasks. Today's adolescents face a similar need to claim their mission within the church's life and faith with the support of family, friends, and community leaders. Young people seek and need the opportunity to question and listen to leaders of the community. Sometimes their need for self-identity and sense of purpose is in tension with parents' exercise of responsibility. Still, teens count on the concern, support, and love of family as they take the natural adolescent risks of discovery.

By Establishing Personal Relationships

Teens need to be able to count on the same support from their communities. By giving witness to the Gospel, living communal charity, and actively celebrating the mysteries of Christ, the Christian community becomes a source of faith development. Pastoral leaders must work together to present the parish as welcoming and supportive. Generally, youth perceive the experience of parish through their relationship with the pastor and other people who have immediate contact with teens in catechetical or liturgical roles. The concept of parish identity or mission is less important to youth than the visibility and welcoming attitude of key adults. They develop this perception through one-on-one relationships with significant adults. For example, youth are more likely to participate in liturgical ministries and other areas of parish life if they have established these personal relationships with the leaders. Usually, the greater the number of adults reaching out to teens, the greater the involvement of youth in parish life will be.

Providing Formation and Catechesis for Discipleship

Through Intentional Catechesis

Catechesis is a foundation for the Christian life, and the goal of liturgical catechesis is to "promote an active, conscious, and genuine participation in the liturgy of the church" (*General Catechetical Directory*, no. 25). "Catechesis is intrinsically linked with the whole of liturgical and sacramental activity" (*Catechesi Tradendae, Catechesis in Our Time*, no. 23). Therefore, the fullness of the Church's sacramental life—the sacraments of initiation, healing, and life mission—should be the subject of intentional catechesis for youth.

Through Liturgical Catechesis

Adolescents are also catechized by their experiences of liturgy. Through immersion in the symbols, stories, and rituals of the communal prayer life, adolescents gain not only knowledge but an appreciation of the power of the sacraments. A major barrier to their full conscious and active participation, however, is a lack of understanding of the sacramental symbols and rituals. A specific objective of intentional catechesis for liturgy is to assist teens through reflection and sharing in exploring how liturgical symbols and rituals celebrate their experiences of God and life events.

Through the Community's Response

We are concerned that a pattern of limited participation and involvement in liturgy as teenagers will establish a pattern for their relationship with the Church as adults. Youth have experiences of God beyond liturgy, but if they never feel the liturgy speaks to these experiences or provides direction for their current life issues, how will they expect the liturgy to hold meaning for them in the future? The Christian community must celebrate the paschal mystery manifested in all the generations.

Through Opportunities for Service

Formation and catechesis for liturgy need to be part of a fuller catechesis directed at living the Christian life. Liturgical catechesis is most effective when it is in concert with the experience of community, exploring the Word, and actively working for the spread of the Gospel. Many youth develop an appreciation for the power of liturgy by offering Christian service and working for justice. By encountering Christ in the poor and confronting social issues, youth experience the paschal mystery in deeper ways. Other youth may need to feel the acceptance of peers to understand liturgy's communal nature. Liturgical experiences should be integrated into a variety of activities and events available to youth. Adolescents should always be invited and encouraged to participate in the parish catechetical opportunities open to all.

Through Retreats and Days of Reflection

Liturgy has the power to draw young people into a deeper relationship with God. Yet at times, we may be guilty of placing too much emphasis on Mass with teens. The spiritual life is not confined to participation in the liturgy, and for many adolescents, the symbols and rituals of the liturgy will remain dormant until these teens develop a more active private prayer life. Teens who have not yet developed patterns of personal prayer may find the rituals of liturgy confusing. Others may find it difficult to fully participate in the Sunday assembly until they have first discovered a personal relationship with Christ. Youth retreats, days of reflection, and other opportunities for prayer in groups assist teens in making this connection to the larger faith community and the liturgy.

Through Family Catechesis

The family is the first educator of youth regarding liturgy and the source of their religious life and practices. The family plays a mediating role between a child and the people of God. Parents and extended family members encourage and teach children and youth to pray and to value daily prayer rituals. Through family prayer times and participation in the liturgy as a family, children and youth are given opportunities to celebrate their personal faith in a group setting. Through family celebrations of life events and holidays, the young gain a sense of the importance of tradition, the dynamic of ritual, and their own role in the family.

If the family has an active prayer life, the young will be predisposed as adolescents to deepening that devotion. Developmental issues may cause some teens to abandon prayer for a time because they associate it with parental control, but most return to find a meaningful style of prayer. In these situations, and particularly in families that have not had an active prayer life, the community becomes a significant source of guidance and support as adolescents develop their prayer life. Appreciation of the rituals of liturgy and the need for prayer may come through youth formation activities.

Through a Variety of Faith Experiences

Adolescent catechesis needs to include experience and interaction. It needs to be regular and varied enough to address teens who have had very little contact with the Church as well as those whose families have given them a solid foundation of prayer. Such a plan will help teens understand that there are many paths to discipleship.

Through Catechist Formation

Many religious educators and youth ministers feel ill-prepared to provide intentional Catechesis for youth about liturgy. Though they know the dynamics of effective liturgy from personal experience, they may not have the formal background and training to feel confident leading liturgical Catechesis. Catechetical leaders should seek formation to become more familiar with liturgical principles in order to assist youth in understanding the liturgy and deepening their own prayer life.

Through Collaboration

In a similar way, many pastors, liturgists, and pastoral musicians feel uncomfortable in youth catechetical settings. Though they know the principles and theology of the rites, they may not have the background in effective catechetical methods for teens. Youth will benefit when pastoral and liturgical leaders work with religious educators and youth ministers to establish simple but comprehensive catechetical sessions for liturgy. When appropriate, parents should be included in the preparation and experience of this liturgical catechesis. Opportunities for intergenerational and family-centered catechesis for liturgy could be valuable in revitalizing the Sunday assembly.

Summary
We count on these foundations as we respond to the challenge of inviting youth to worship. We believe that the Spirit has given their gifts to the Church. Through the partnership of family and parish, we discover and affirm those gifts. Through effective Catechesis, we develop the fullness of those gifts. Through the liturgy, we celebrate those gifts in our midst.

Principles for Vibrant Worship with Adolescents

Vibrant Worship with Adolescents Celebrates Their Involvement in the Church's Life and Mission

Liturgy is grounded in the life of Jesus and in the Church's experience of Christ. Liturgy celebrates our participation in the Mystical Body of Christ at work in the world. It is our lives that first give praise to the Creator. Without the experience of living the Christian life, liturgy can be an empty ritual for adolescents. Therefore, all the ways in which the Church ministers to its youth and involves them in an active Christian lifestyle help to make the liturgy a more vibrant celebration for teens. Through a comprehensive youth ministry, youth are more ready to greet Christ present in Word and Sacrament.

To respond effectively to the diversity of its young people, the local community needs faithful adults willing to minister to and with adolescents in a variety of settings. Peer ministries are also important to creating a comprehensive youth ministry. All these efforts work together to help youth understand that "the liturgy is the summit toward which the activity of the Church is directed; at the same time it is the font from which all her power flows" (*Sacred Liturgy*, no. 10).

Being an adolescent in today's media-dominated culture is difficult and different from the experiences of previous generations. We trust in the Spirit of Christ to "manifest the faith and show forth its newness in cultures which have been secularized and desacralized" (*General Catechetical Directory*, no. 5). We need to hear the stories of struggle and joy of being a Catholic Christian in the schools, neighborhoods, and work places of this generation. We want to stand with youth and support them in living the Christian life.

Parishes and Catholic schools demonstrate this principle by:

- encouraging youth to join with adults and their peers in activities for service and justice in the larger community;
- providing opportunities for youth to celebrate liturgy related to service and justice activities;
- acknowledging these experiences more directly in the parish worship;
- encouraging youth to exercise their natural leadership gifts and talents.

Vibrant Worship with Adolescents Invites and Accepts Their Authentic Participation

Authentic participation implies that adolescence is a natural and necessary stage of life and that adolescents are important and necessary to the community's understanding and celebration of the presence of Christ in its midst. Authentic participation by adolescents is varied and can seem childlike as well as adultlike in its expression. The range of responses can include both the stereotypically disinterested teen present at liturgy because of parents' insistence and the accomplished young musician who accompanies the parish choir every week. Authentic participation expresses the true faith experiences of youth, at whatever stage of development that faith may be, and as witness to their full, conscious, and active Christian lifestyles.

The liturgical setting is also a factor in youth participation. Some youth may experience the power of liturgy more authentically in peer groups. Others may need the support of parents and significant adults to encourage their understanding and participation in parish liturgies. Of course, some youth will remain indifferent to the liturgy despite our best efforts to include them. There are many paths by which adolescents can experience the presence of Christ in communal prayer. Therefore, a balanced approach to promoting authentic youth participation includes a variety of options. We must trust that the grace of the Holy Spirit is at work in all the baptized, though at times it is not visible to us.

Not all youth possess the charisms to be liturgical ministers, but all youth need formation to understand the ministry of the assembly. There are some youth in every parish who are ready and eager for regular involvement in the liturgical ministries. The awareness, skills, and abilities that are naturally present in all teens need nurturing and development to come to their fullness. We have learned to respect adolescents' natural developmental abilities in education and athletics. Students and athletes are given gradually increasing responsibilities. A similar approach, one that respects natural gifts and age-related abilities, is needed for youth participation in the liturgical ministries. Young people who exercise these ministries become signs of encouragement to their peers and signs of God's continuing renewal of the church.

Parishes and Catholic schools demonstrate this principle by:
- acknowledging youth faith issues at all liturgies in ways appropriate to the rites;
- providing opportunities for youth to be trained as liturgical ministers;
- scheduling periodic liturgies at youth events prepared with youth input;
- inviting youth to help prepare the community liturgies.

Vibrant Worship with Adolescents Attends to the Diversity of Ages and Cultures in the Assembly

Respect for cultures and inclusion of local art, music, and expressions are visible in vibrant worship. Those who prepare liturgy need to be familiar with the diversity of races, cultures, and ages of those present in the assembly. The prayers, songs, and symbols need to be prepared knowing that "the Church respects and fosters the genius and talents of the various races and peoples" (*Sacred Liturgy*, no. 37).

All liturgy takes place within a cultural context. Contemporary culture provides a context in which today's adolescents perceive symbols, scripture, and rituals. The rites need to reflect this diversity of cultures by examples, musical styles, decor, and references to current events. "We feel ourselves called to reach out beyond our nationalities, races, languages and socio-economic levels, so as to be really one Catholic family" (USCCB, compendium of *The Hispanic Presence, National Pastoral Plan for Hispanic Ministry,* and *Prophetic Voices,* p. 41). We sensitively use the expressions of all cultures not out of tokenism but in a spirit of solidarity with a diverse church and as a recognition of the gifts the Spirit has provided. Adolescents were raised as members of a "global village," and they can help the rest of the assembly to become aware of the cultural dynamics celebrated in the liturgy.

Adolescents are a distinct age group in our society and culture. Their language expressions, musical preferences, and ways of life are often quite different from those of the other generations. Those who prepare the liturgy need to find appropriate ways to incorporate the youth culture's idioms into worship, remembering that "the pastoral effectiveness of a celebration will be heightened if the texts of the readings, prayers, and songs correspond as closely as possible to the needs, religious dispositions, and aptitude of the participants" (USCCB, *General Instruction of the Roman Missal,* no. 313).

Parishes and Catholic schools demonstrate this principle by:

- exploring new music, song texts, and service music being composed for liturgy;
- inviting youth to act as cultural resources—informing liturgy committees about current "signs of the times" that could be incorporated in the prayers, songs, or rituals;
- giving youth experiences of other cultural worship styles so that they can gain a greater appreciation for their own.

Vibrant Worship with Adolescents Roots and Fosters Their Personal Prayer Relationship with God

The Church professes the mystery of faith in the Creed and celebrates it in the sacramental liturgy, and the faithful "live it in a vital and personal relationship with the living and true God. This relationship is prayer" (*Catechism of the Catholic Church,* no. 2558). When we pray, we respond to God's gift of faith and open ourselves to the power of God's covenant love. In prayer, we are united—in communion—with the whole church. We have a duty, therefore, to foster the development of a personal prayer life in the young and to celebrate the ritual moments of their daily lives in prayer.

The symbols and rituals of liturgy become more meaningful for youth when they draw from their experiences of private prayer. Likewise, meaningful experiences of the liturgy revitalize private prayer. Opportunities for prayer in peer, family, and intergenerational settings allow youth to experience the fullness of prayer styles in the church's tradition. As youth discover and develop their own prayer expression, they often become more willing to participate in the parish assembly. For this reason, youth leaders and catechists need to provide a variety of traditional and contemporary prayer experiences for and with youth.

Pastoral leaders should avoid praying at youth rather than praying with youth. Too often group prayer becomes a matter of reading from printed sheets and paying little attention to current events and issues in young peoples' lives. Teens need opportunities and encouragement to voice spontaneous prayers, sing in groups, and bring their ideas and issues to community prayer. These experiences lead the way to greater participation in the liturgy. Adolescents also benefit from periodic prayer opportunities with their families and other adults. The Church can foster and develop family prayer in this way.

The liturgy of the hours, liturgies of reconciliation and healing, and ritual devotions such as the stations of the cross, allow for creativity and adaptation to the life issues and cultural expressions of youth. When these liturgies are primarily for teens, the music selections, prayers, symbols, and gestures can be more contemporary and youth-oriented. More youth can also be involved in the preparation and ministries.

Parishes and Catholic schools demonstrate this principle by:
- scheduling seasonal prayer events for youth;
- involving teens in the preparation of prayer experiences for their peers;
- providing family prayer resources;
- including personal prayer time within all youth events and catechetical sessions.

Vibrant Worship
Includes Effective Preaching of the Word

Quality preaching is the number one issue named by youth when they are asked what makes liturgy meaningful. They regularly mention storytelling and the use of examples that relate to their own situation in life as effective techniques for preaching. The homilist's sense of humor can help teens connect the homily to their life experiences. Visualizations and scenarios also help the Word come alive for the whole assembly.

Effective preaching encourages the young to further explore and study the relevance of the Scriptures for this day and age. In the process, parents and other family members will also better understand how the gospel might be lived in family settings where adolescents are present. "By means of the homily the mysteries of the faith and the guiding principles of the Christian life are expounded from the sacred text" (*Sacred Liturgy*, no. 52).

Youth ministers and youth peer leaders can help pastors and others who preach the Word by suggesting examples, stories, and anecdotes that the preacher can use or reflect upon when developing homilies. There are, however, two preliminary steps. First, a supportive relationship with the *homilists* must be established to encourage trust and their openness to youthful expressions. Second, the homilist must invite teens to share their faith stories in a way that respects confidentiality. No young person is going to truthfully discuss peer relationships or situations if there is the possibility of being embarrassed. We know that Jesus used the ordinary situations and symbols of people's lives to preach effectively. We must do the same.

Parishes and Catholic schools demonstrate this principle by:
- inviting youth to reflect on the seasonal readings and to offer connections to their lives;
- providing regular opportunities for youth to study the Scriptures;
- encouraging those who preach to use current examples and storytelling techniques;
- investigating the developments within culture for their impact on youths' vernacular.

Vibrant Worship
Has a Youthful Spirit in Music and Song

The Church clarified that all musical styles, especially the music of the people, are to be considered for worship while respecting the functional needs of song within the rites. The people's own religious songs are to be encouraged with care so that "the faithful may raise their voices in song" (adapted from *Sacred Liturgy*, no. 118). Music is a significant part of personal expression for youth and that expression carries over to their participation in liturgy. The music of the young brings freshness and variety to our current musical genres and can infuse sacred music with energy and vitality.

Though the music of the liturgy has the power to unite us symbolically in common song, there is much tension in our parishes regarding musical styles. Everyone, young and old, has a favorite musical style. The function of music at liturgy, however, is to support the community prayer, not to entertain. This is sometimes difficult for teens to understand. Pastoral musicians have a difficult task balancing the threefold judgment described in *Music in Catholic Worship*—liturgical, musical, and pastoral—when choosing music for worship.

The Church has a rich tradition of sacred music, and that has been expanded by the contemporary liturgical music written since the council. Sacred music, by definition, is music old and new that turns our ears and attention to the Creator. "Thus the church remains faithful in its responsibility as a teacher of truth to guard 'things old' at the same time . . . bringing forth 'things new' (see Mt 13:52)" (USCCB, *General Instruction of the Roman Missal*, no. 13). We have a responsibility to invite youth to appreciate a variety of traditional and contemporary liturgical music styles.

The primary function of liturgical music is participation, but it is music's performance by the assembly that captures our imaginations and moves us to participation. Young people say that much of today's liturgical music does not captivate their hearts or ears. They respond as much to the way the music is performed and styled as they do to the actual melodies and texts. When music is played with enthusiasm, a variety of instrumentation, and an upbeat pace, they are more likely to participate. Pastoral leaders should be aware, however, that sometimes youth do not sing just because their peers do not, and the lack of participation has little to do with the music itself. By allowing youth to bring their musical genius to our assembly, we encourage them to value and appreciate the fullness of our sacred musical heritage.

Parishes and Catholic schools demonstrate this principle by:
- inviting youth to participate in the choirs and musical ensembles;
- exploring contemporary accompaniments and focusing on music's *sound and pace;*
- expanding the repertoire of hymns and songs to include youth selections;
- encouraging assembly singing so that youth feel comfortable adding their voices.

Vibrant Worship Incorporates Visually Dynamic Symbols and Actions

The liturgy and sacraments depend upon "signs perceptible to the senses" (*Sacred Liturgy*, no. 7). We have an obligation to assess how "perceptible" our preparation of the symbols and symbolic actions of the liturgy are. Our current culture conditions us to watch passively what goes on around us. Sometimes this passivity is at odds with the dynamic of liturgy that calls for active involvement and acclamation. Furthermore, the renewal of the liturgy set forth by the Second Vatican Council recognized that "art of our own days, coming from every race and region, shall also be given free scope in the Church, provided that it adorns the sacred buildings and holy rites with due reverence and honor" (*Sacred Liturgy*, no. 123). Both these issues affect the liturgical experiences of youth.

Today's youth have been educated through multimedia. Their visual sense is their primary way of learning and responding to their environment. Their level of visual literacy usually exceeds their parents' and elders' abilities. They become bored when the visual nature of the rites is weak. At liturgy we more often rely upon our ears for song texts, proclamation of the Word, homily, acclamations, and prayers, and our eyes are disengaged. It would not be an understatement to say that when teens' eyes are not active, their brains shut down. We say that not in judgment but because that is how youth relate to the world. Unless their eyes are engaged, they may find it difficult to comprehend or appreciate the ritual.

Youth need education to develop their own prayer response within liturgy. Liturgy, by its nature, has moments of silence and opportunities for meditation that allow us to recall interior experiences and images. These prayerful "daydreams" are important dimensions of the full liturgical experience. They often form the basis of our personal response to the liturgy. Opportunities for private reflection and meditation outside the liturgy will also help teens to develop these prayer skills.

We must provide catechesis about the meaning of the symbols and rites. Youth are at a severe disadvantage when the symbols are static, small, or otherwise poorly prepared. In prayer settings with youth, youth ministers have found that processions, simple movements and gestures, candles, colors, artwork, and lighting all contribute to youth participation. A variety of media should be appropriately integrated into the rites and should not be added to the liturgy as a gimmick to attract adolescents.

Parishes and Catholic schools demonstrate this principle by:

- inviting youth to assess the visual dynamics of the liturgical rituals and symbols;
- providing visual aids (for example, orders of worship, copies of the readings in catechetical sessions, and so forth) to encourage youth participation;
- exploring the appropriate use of media at liturgy.

Vibrant Worship
Has an Interactive and Communal Dimension

"Liturgical services are not private functions, but celebrations of the Church" (*Sacred Liturgy*, no. 26). As we develop our approach to liturgy as a celebration of the whole community—rather than a time for collective, individual devotion and prayer—we will assist youth in entering into the experience of liturgy. Teens want to belong. They want to feel welcomed. They are very sensitive to the hospitality displayed at liturgy.

By their nature, adolescents seek identity through their groups. Their natural affinity for group expression and celebration can be a gift to our worshiping assemblies. Sometimes their attendance in groups is intimidating to adults. Youth who tend to isolate themselves in their peer groups need to be challenged to experience also the family's and community's expression of prayer.

Presiders and other ministers have a significant role in determining how the young experience group worship. For example, the presider's use of an introductory comment may help acclimate an assembly that is newly gathered or new to him. It is important that these ministers let their personal sense of faith influence the exercising of their roles. Young people notice. A sense of humor, a warm smile, a personal anecdote, even the admission of error when things go awry are small but significant ways to engage youth.

The youngest generations have also been raised in very interactive media environments. They expect to touch, select, and respond to computer and animated situations. How can we help them to transfer this wonderful ability to other people and the community when it prays? Youth may lead us in an understanding of the global liturgical connectivity.

Parishes and Catholic schools demonstrate this principle by:
- focusing on the hospitality provided at liturgy;
- encouraging teens to liturgy with their friends;
- building a sense of community among youth before liturgy;
- ministering in a personal way;
- affirming the presence and involvement of teens whenever possible.

Strategies for Renewal

Begin the Conversation Locally

We encourage committees, priests, liturgists, musicians, religious educators, parents, youth ministers, and other pastoral leaders to gather with youth and discuss ways in which local liturgies might become more vibrant for teens. This document can assist local dioceses, parishes, and campuses to begin that discussion. The most important strategy is the conversation itself. No plan will succeed without the dialogue that leads to a collaborative effort. Young people understand the value of working together.

Youth want to be included in the conversation. They understand the value of tradition, but they also want their issues to be given due consideration. Liturgical leaders should not be troubled when teens question the reasoning behind some liturgical practices. This is a necessary part of their coming to understand the dynamics of liturgy. Patient explanations of the liturgical principles will help encourage youth to add their creativity in ways consistent with the tradition. At the same time, their questioning may help keep local practices in line with liturgical norms and make celebrations more vibrant for all the members of the assembly. Many young people feel uncomfortable being alone in the company of a group of adults. They look for the familiarity and security of peer companionship. Invite teens *personally* and identify the specific reasons why they are being invited and what talents or perspectives are being sought.

The local context is important to consider. Plans for improving the experience of worship for teens will be best when they take into account the characteristics and history of the local parish, campus, or civic community. The environments in which youth work, recreate, and are educated also need to be considered.

Above all, keep Christ at the center of the conversation. It is too easy to get so focused on music, preaching, and other liturgical issues that we overlook the overall purpose of liturgy. All of our efforts must ultimately be directed toward helping young people deepen their faith and be part of the community as it expresses its faith in Christ and in one another.

Listen to Youth

We encourage local pastoral leaders to listen to the issues teens in their community raise. Teens in your area may be experiencing particular joys or difficulties that need to be heard. An effective pastoral plan will be responsive to these local issues and involve youth in considering solutions.

Listen to a variety of young people, including those who have almost no current contact with the parish. No adult, not even those more recently out of high school, is able adequately to represent the perspective of current teens. It may be necessary to reach beyond the current parish roster to obtain these other perspectives.

Reaching out to these youth may also renew parish evangelization efforts.

Listening is fundamental to the ongoing renewal of the liturgy for all the members of the assembly. Identifying the specific needs of adolescents should be balanced by seeking the ideas from other identifiable groups. Youth needs and concerns may not be widely different from other parish members' needs. A more balanced pastoral plan has a greater chance for acceptance by the full parish than a plan specifically addressed to youth.

Paying attention to youth is vital to collaboration. Take teens' opinions seriously, however. Youth can articulate their issues but will need time and assurance that their voice is important. Youth ministers, parents, grandparents, and other adults need to serve as advocates in this process.

Apprentice Youth in the Liturgical Ministries / Promote the Call to Ministry

Pastoral and liturgical leaders need to provide a welcome and safe environment in which teens can offer their gifts and enthusiasm. Many adolescents want to be involved in the ministries, but many will not volunteer without being asked or even gently persuaded.

Establishing apprenticeships for the liturgical ministries is one highly effective approach. Youth are paired with established liturgical ministers for training and actually engaging in the ministry. The goal of apprenticing is larger than simply involving some youth in ministry. In the apprenticeship process, positive relationships between adults and youth are developed. These relationships provide a larger base of support for ongoing youth involvement in parish life. An adult parish leader who has had a positive experience of working with one young person is likely to have a more favorable attitude toward other youth.

Every parish ministry and organization can benefit from the creativity, idealism, and enthusiasm of teens. Likewise, youth who have established personal relationships with adult leaders can develop closer ties with the parish. An effective parish will help its members make the connections between worship and work; between liturgy and life in the family, community, and work place" (USCCB, *Called and Gifted for the Third Millennium*, p. 15).

If parishes state clearly and simply what tasks and skills are needed, then teens can make a personal choice to become lectors, greeters, musicians, singers, and eucharistic ministers. Some teens will need direction in identifying the skills they can provide. Others still have not developed the self-esteem to know they are capable of serving. Parents, grandparents, and other adult members of the parish are the best advocates in this process.

Some youth may be too shy to accept at first but will respond if you are appropriately persistent and personal. Ask again. Some youth may currently be involved in a school production or sport and be unable to accept your invitation. Keep in mind that "long range" for adolescents is more often measured in weeks and months than in years.

Sometimes our understanding of the call to ministry is limited to vocations to the priesthood and religious life. The church, however, continues to need people to serve as full-time liturgists, liturgical musicians, religious educators, and other pastoral leaders. Adolescents need to be made aware of the variety of parish ministries that can benefit from their efforts, and those who possess the desire to pursue these life vocations should be encouraged and supported. Financial support for participation in local, regional, and national leadership events is critical. Providing volunteers to accompany these teens also demonstrates parish support.

Celebrate Liturgies at Youth Events Well

Liturgies celebrated primarily for and with adolescents occur within the context of retreats, days of reflection, or other youth events in the parish, diocese, or region. These events provide an opportunity to pay great attention to the life experiences and issues young people bring to worship. The prayers, music, homily, and liturgical decor can be more specifically directed toward youth. More teens can be involved in the liturgical ministries, and more emphasis can be placed on the ministry of the assembly from a youth perspective.

Youth are catechized by their liturgical experiences. Whether mass, reconciliation, or the sacrament of healing, these liturgies can be moments when the liturgical symbols and rituals take on greater meaning because a sense of community and prayer has been developed. "Faith grows when it is well expressed in celebration. Good celebrations foster and nourish faith. Poor celebrations may weaken and destroy it" (Bishops' Committee on the Liturgy, *Music in Catholic Worship*, p. 1).

Pastoral, liturgical, and catechetical leaders need to prepare these liturgies well so they increase the hunger in youth for meeting Christ in the Sunday assembly and in other parish worship settings. Many youth simply feel more comfortable praying in a group of peers, and these events may be their first step toward experiencing the communal nature of liturgy beyond their immediate family.

Provide Opportunities for Youth Involvement in Sunday Worship

As we stated in our purpose, very often teens are absent from or disinterested in Sunday mass. Consequently, some youth leaders ask whether parishes should schedule a separate youth mass every week. However, Sunday mass is the prayer of the whole Body of Christ, and, therefore, the assembly should never be limited to one age group or another. Occasionally, masses at separate youth events (see the previous strategy) occur on Sundays. In these circumstances, the group joins the full church by celebrating the normal Sunday or feast. A weekly, *youth-only* mass can discourage youth from experiencing the prayer of the whole church and can isolate teens from their families. The visibility and charisms of young people are lost to the faith community when youth are gathered on their own every week. A more effective strategy is to consider ways that young people can be encouraged to participate in all masses.

Some parishes have bridged this concern by designating a regularly scheduled Sunday mass (often Sunday evening) as a liturgy that features increased youth involvement in the ministries and a style of music that is more contemporary. This allows families to worship together and the rest of the parish to be included, while offering teens the opportunity to worship with a greater number of their peers. Some parishes schedule religious education or social events in conjunction with these masses.

Pray to the Holy Spirit

Above all, we encourage all who would advocate for young people to count on the presence and power of the Holy Spirit to renew the church. Never cease praying that God's grace will be bestowed upon the young in full measure. By remaining open to that Spirit, the best paths for local renewal will be discerned.

Conclusion

> A major challenge for the third millennium is to bring our Catholic tradition to life in the hearts, minds and spirits of new generations. No one does this alone; God's grace is the context and the means. All are called to the task of handing on the faith of our mothers and fathers, of the martyrs and saints. (*Called and Gifted*, p. 21)

The challenge of worship with adolescents involves gathering all the generations with a renewed sense of the power of liturgy. The foundation of our efforts is our role as youth advocates. As youth ministers, catechists, religious educators, priests, liturgists, pastoral ministers, and administrators, we support families and parishes in providing liturgical formation to the young. We walk with them as they encounter the height and depth, length and breadth of God's love.

There is, therefore, really only one challenge from age to age: to be faithful witnesses of God's power and presence in the world and in our lives. We believe that the Spirit of the risen Christ encounters us through the youth in our midst. They challenge us to grow and to be open to that Spirit. As we celebrate that sacred mystery with youth, we give thanks to God for their vitality and charisms. We accept the challenge and invite all to join us in this adventure toward renewal.

Chapter 3

The Challenge of Adolescent Catechesis:
Maturing in Faith

Introduction

All human beings experience change during adolescence. This change can be exciting if it awakens a deeper sense of self-identity, leads to the expansion of authentic freedom, enhances our ability to relate to others, and promotes greater maturity. However, the changes of adolescence can also be depressing, alienating, and filled with self-doubt and anxiety. Precisely because of the many divergent possibilities, the time of adolescence is a unique opportunity for the Catholic Christian community to affirm, support, and challenge young people to grow as persons and believers.

Over the past decade, the Church has developed an all-embracing approach to ministry with youth. As articulated in *A Vision of Youth Ministry* (USCCB, 1986), this comprehensive approach to youth recognizes their personal, familial, social, and spiritual needs and the environments that affect their lives. It also invites them into the life, mission, and work of the faith community. In the past 10 years, a coordinated, multi-dimensional ministry of the Word, worship, justice/service, community life, guidance/healing, enablement, and advocacy has evolved in parishes and schools to respond to the needs of today's youth. The ongoing evangelization and catechesis of youth are essential and integral elements of fostering the maturing in faith of the "Young Church of Today."

Adolescent catechesis is clearly in a state of transition, reflecting both the cultural and ecclesial shifts of the past two decades. The growth of catechetical theory and practice and the evolution of the Church's ministry with youth have forced church leaders to rethink adolescent catechesis, to clarify its aim and scope, and to recognize its contribution within the broader context of ministry. Moreover, the dramatic increase in the number of coordinators of youth ministry and high school campus ministry has resulted in confusion and tension regarding responsibilities for adolescent catechesis at every level of the Church—schools, parishes, and diocesan offices. This changing and somewhat perplexing scene presents the Church with a marvelous opportunity to develop new initiatives in vision and practice that will shape adolescent catechesis.

This paper is a serious and cooperative effort to speak in a fresh way to the needs and gifts of young people and to determine how the Church can respond to those needs and affirm those gifts through effective catechesis. God's Word when proclaimed, celebrated, shared, and lived in the Christian community is dynamic and fruitful. What an opportunity exists when the energy and giftedness of young people can be engaged with the vibrancy and richness of God's Word! The possibilities for personal development and growth in faith are then enormous and can lead to a richer life for the entire Catholic Christian community and for the family. The enthusiasm and challenge offered by young people who become more involved in the life of the Church can energize parish, home, and society.

The opportunity of engaging adolescents in the life of the Church challenges us. As youth experience and express their expanding freedom, they resist mediocre or halfhearted efforts. Effective catechesis with youth requires that the adult members of our community grow continually in their faith and in their ability to share it with others. This growth is especially necessary for the parents of adolescents. We cannot expect more of youth than we do of adults. The ways we adults learn about, express, and live out faith is a vigorous support or a serious obstacle in effectively catechizing youth.

This paper is addressed to leaders in ministry with youth and in catechetical ministry in parishes, Catholic schools, and diocesan offices. It is written to affirm, support, and encourage the creative initiatives of ministers with youth across this country and to challenge the Church in the United States to take seriously its catechetical ministry with the "Young Church of Today." By proposing the aim, process, and principles for adolescent catechesis and a framework of key faith themes for younger and older adolescents, and by identifying the roles and responsibilities of key leaders in ministry with youth, the paper sets forth a vision and direction for adolescent catechesis.

The Foundations of Adolescent Catechesis

The Ministry of Adolescent Catechesis is rooted in the Church's understanding and experience of six foundational themes: Jesus, discipleship, mission and ministries, faith, the developing human person, and the community.

. . . Rooted in Jesus Christ

The essence of Christian faith is a living relationship with God—a God fully revealed by Jesus of Nazareth and present to us through the Holy Spirit. This Spirit fills and transforms the lives of his followers. When people encountered Jesus' sustaining love and transforming power they experienced the saving love of God. The very person of Jesus made the saving love of God accessible. The life, death, and resurrection of Jesus of Nazareth is the Revelation of God. If we want to learn how to relate to God, we focus on the person of Jesus—his life and message, his death and resurrection. A Christian disciple lives in relationship with God in Jesus Christ.

. . . Rooted in Christian Discipleship

"Jesus came to Galilee proclaiming the good news of God, and saying, 'The time is fulfilled, and the kingdom of God has come near; repent, and believe in the good news' (Mark 1:14–15).

The Gospel of Jesus is the Good News of the reign of God. Jesus used the image of the reign of God or the kingdom of God to reveal God's presence among people and God's promises for them. Jesus proclaimed the reign in his words and made it present in his actions. He called people to conversion and repentance. He asked them to turn away from sin, from all that bound and oppressed them and to turn toward faith and freedom. Jesus invited people to believe in, trust in, and live the Good News. Those who accepted the invitation experienced a new life—a life faithful to the values and vision of the reign of God.

Through his teachings, Jesus described the character, priorities, values, and norms of the reign of God. Jesus addressed the fundamental questions that each of us must face. Jesus summons us to journey with him. The relationship to which he calls us defines us as his disciples—people who belong to the Lord and serve God alone. The first disciples joined Jesus, followed him, transferred their loyalty to him, and, in so doing, became a new people.

The first disciples shared in the mission of Jesus. While essential to the Christian experience, discipleship is costly, for the invitation to follow Jesus and to share in his mission demands total response and requires a lifelong conversion. Accepting the values and priorities of the reign of God forces us to break with many of the values of our culture. Only the power of grace can effect this profound social and personal transformation.

The Good News of Jesus and the dynamics of Christian Discipleship are the energizing core of the catechesis. "At the heart of catechesis, we find, in essence, a Person, the Person of Jesus of Nazareth" (*Catechesis in Our Time,* no. 5). Our catechetical task "has the twofold objective of maturing the initial faith and of educating the true disciple of Christ by means of a deeper and more systematic knowledge of the person and message of our Lord Jesus Christ" (no. 19).

. . . Rooted in the Church's Mission and Ministries

The spirit of the Lord is upon me,
    because he has anointed me
        to bring good news to the poor.
He has sent me to proclaim release to the captives
    and recovery of sight to the blind,
        to let the oppressed go free,
to proclaim the year of the Lord's favor.

(Luke 4:18–19)

Through the power and presence of the Holy Spirit, the mission of Jesus is continued in the Church. Faithful to the mission of Jesus, the Church is called to proclaim in word and in sacrament the definitive arrival of the Kingdom in Jesus of Nazareth; to offer itself as a sign of its own proclamation—to be a people transformed by the Spirit into a community of faith, and facilitate the coming of the reign of God through service within the community of faith and in the world at large.

Four fundamental ministries that have their roots in the life of Jesus serve the mission of the Church: ministry of the Word, the ministry of community building, the ministry of worship, and the ministry of serving-healing. Each of these ministries continues the work of Jesus. "The ministry of the Word takes many forms, among them evangelization or missionary preaching, catechesis, liturgy, and theology" (adapted from the Sacred Congregation for the Clergy, *General Catechetical Directory*, no. 17). An integral element of the ministry of the Word is catechesis.

Catechesis—Linked with the Other Ministries

All ministries have catechetical aspects. "Catechesis is intrinsically linked with the whole of liturgical and sacramental activity, for it is in the sacraments, especially in the Eucharist, that Christ Jesus works in fullness for the transformation of human beings" (*Catechesis in Our Time,* no. 23). "Catechesis is closely linked with the responsible activity of the Church and of Christians in the world. . . . If catechesis is done well, Christians will be eager to bear witness to their faith, to hand it on to their children, to make it known to others, and to serve the human community in every way" (no. 24).

The interrelationship of catechesis with the other ministries of the Church is reflected in *A Vision of Youth Ministry*, which describes adolescent catechesis as one component of a multi-dimensional ministry with youth. Each component of this multi-dimensional ministry fosters maturing in faith.

Catechesis—A Responsibility of the Community

Responsibility for catechesis rests with the entire Church. "Catechesis always has been and always will be a work for which the whole Church must feel responsible and must wish to be responsible" (*Catechesis in Our Time,* no. 16). The entire faith community needs to be interested in, supportive of, and concerned about adolescent catechesis.

Catechesis and Evangelization

This paper elaborates an understanding and practice of catechesis as a systematic, planned, and intentional pastoral

activity. This activity is directed toward the kind of teaching and learning which emphasizes growth in Christian faith through understanding, reflection, and transformation (cf. *Catechesis in Our Time,* nos. 19 and 21). Although catechesis is a broad reality, this paper focuses on that aspect of catechesis that is systematic and intentional and that can be planned.

Catechesis is closely related to evangelization, which is the energizing core of all ministries. All ministries are elements in the evangelization/conversion process. As an evangelizing activity, catechesis promotes an ongoing conversion toward a permanent commitment to the Lord. "Within the whole process of evangelization, the aim of catechesis is to be the teaching and maturation stage" (*Catechesis in Our Time,* no. 20).

In a time when so many young people remain untouched by the Good News, initial evangelization is a priority. Through evangelization we invite young people into the community of faith, into a faith relationship with Jesus Christ, and into the lifestyle of the Good News. Catechesis then builds upon this faith by explaining more fully the Good News and by exploring the common faith that binds that Catholic Christian community together. Catechesis seeks to foster the maturing of faith of young people.

. . . Rooted in Christian Faith

Christian faith is a gift of God inviting people to a living relationship with God in Jesus Christ. In the years since Vatican II, the Church has reiterated its belief that faith has affective (trusting), cognitive (believing), and behavioral (doing) dimensions. We remain firmly convinced that Christian faith must be lived. Catechesis that takes the Christian faith as its purpose intentionally promotes all three dimensions—trusting, believing, and doing (cf. Thomas H. Groome, *Christian Religious Education: Sharing Our Story and Vision* [San Francisco: Harper and Row, 1980], pages 84–103).

An Activity of Trusting

Christian faith is a response to an invitation to a loyal and trusting relationship with God. Developing and deepening the adolescent's relationship with God in Jesus requires particular attention to and catechesis on the activity of personal and communal prayer. Catechesis attempts to dispose young people to awe, reverence, and wonder at the goodness of God. The loving relationship adolescents develop with God will shape and be shaped by their relationship with other people. The affective dimension of the Christian faith helps young people develop and deepen their sense of belonging within the faith community. Catechesis has the task of enabling adolescents to develop friendship-making and maintenance skills. Such a catechesis seeks to promote in adolescents a deep and abiding bond of friendship and good will toward the whole human family.

An Activity of Believing

The cognitive dimension of Christian faith—the activity of believing—requires that we provide opportunities for youth to deepen and expand their understanding of the scriptural/doctrinal expression of our faith tradition in ways appropriate to their readiness and maturity. We do this by showing the reasonableness of assenting to Catholic Christian beliefs, by helping youth draw on the wisdom of Catholic Christian tradition to give meaning to their lives, and by enabling youth to think for themselves about matters of faith. We help them to articulate their understanding of the tradition in a language appropriate to their generation (cf. *General Catechetical Directory*, no. 88).

An Activity of Doing

Christian faith requires a catechesis that promotes a life based on the values of the reign of God. This means that we present the Christian story as Good News, thus enabling young people to live as a Christian people—joyfully, hopefully, peacefully, and justly. Catechesis challenges young people to respond to God's love by living a life of loving service to others and by working for peace and justice on all levels of human existence—the personal, the interpersonal, and the social/political. The "doing of faith" leads to a deepening of faith. Faith leads to doing and doing leads to renewed faith.

. . . Rooted in the Developing Human Person

A social and developmental understanding of the human person guides our ministry with youth. Through this ministry we seek to create a climate conducive to the healthy development of adolescents and providing them with multiple opportunities for growth in maturity. We want to help them interact with peers, acquire a sense of belonging, and develop self-worth and a healthy self-concept. They need to gain experience in decision making, discuss diverse values, and formulate their own value system. We are challenged to help them explore different understandings of personal and vocational identity, to voice openly their questions in the area of sexuality, to develop a sense of accountability in the context of relationships, and to cultivate a capacity to enjoy life (cf. USCCB, *Sharing the Light of Faith*, no. 180).

Maturing in Christian faith is a lifelong journey for everyone. It is a process of conversion, not a point of arrival. Adolescents are at a crucial point in this lifelong journey. While younger adolescents build their faith identity upon the beliefs, attitudes, and values of the Christian community, older adolescents are beginning to reflect critically on the community's faith, seeking to establish a personally-owned faith identity. They are beginning to take seriously the burden of responsibility for their own commitments, lifestyle, beliefs, and attitudes. The journey from accepting the faith of the community to owning their own faith within the community is often a time of deeper questioning and of anguished or even frustrating searching (cf. *Catechesis in Our Time*, no. 38). It is a crucial time of maturing. "Catechesis cannot ignore these changeable aspects of this delicate period of life" (no. 38). In fact, adolescent catechesis must view adolescents as maturing people who are experiencing their own questions, joys, struggles, and quests for meaning. Adolescent catechesis helps young people understand the relationship of Jesus and the Church to the important realities in their lives (cf. *Sharing the Light of Faith*, no. 174).

. . . Rooted in Christian Community

The call of Jesus was to a new commitment and a new companionship. The earliest Christians were a community of faith, sharing a new way of life:

> They devoted themselves to the apostles' teaching and fellowship, to the breaking of bread and the prayers. . . . Day by day, as they spent much time together in the temple, they broke bread at home and ate their food with glad and generous hearts, praising God and having the goodwill of all the people.

And day by day the Lord added to their number those who were being saved. (Acts 2:42–47)

They were known for the way they lived as well as what they believed. Their experience continues today. The Christian faith produces a discernible lifestyle, a way of life, a process of growth visible to all, a community of believers. The context for catechesis is this faith community.

This community shapes our self-identity. Within this community, we encounter role models, a world view, and a value system that we can interiorize as our own Catholic Christian self-identity. These Catholic Christian environments include the family, the parish, ethnic culture, and ministry with youth in parishes and Catholic schools.

The Family

The family serves the life and mission of the Church by becoming an evangelizing and catechizing community (cf. *Familiaris Consortio*, nos. 51–54, at *www.vatican.va/holy_father/john_paul_ii/ apost_exhortations/documents/hf_jp-ii_exh_19811122_familiaris-consortio_en.html*, accessed October 14, 2004). Family relationships can support or hinder the faith growth of the young person. Moreover, family members catechize informally but powerfully. Parents strengthen the faith of adolescents in many ways—by showing love and affection, by nurturing their adolescents, by living their Catholic Christian moral beliefs, by responding to the needs of others and working for peace and justice, by helping their adolescents internalize moral beliefs, by developing a liberating rather than a restrictive faith life, by sharing their experiences of faith with members of the family, by discussing Scripture and praying with the family, and by reverently receiving the Eucharist and living its spirit (cf. *Sharing the Light of Faith*, no. 212).

Frequently stress, caused by separation or divorce, by living in a single parent or blended family, by unemployment or illness, or by family disunity, affects growth in faith. Adolescent catechesis acknowledges the varied family styles in the United States and the particular stresses experienced by the contemporary family and responds with new directions and strategies. Many parents recognize their need for assistance in fostering the faith of their adolescent children. When adolescents test their independence from the family, other adults may assist parents by serving as Christian role models. A family perspective needs to be woven throughout adolescent catechesis. Acknowledging the importance of the family in catechesis means sponsoring programs for parents around their areas of need, creating parent catechetical experiences that parallel the adolescent catechetical program, sponsoring intergenerational catechetical experiences, and supporting parents in their catechetical ministry. The Church of the Home needs to reclaim its own mission and task. Once this happens, the parish can initiate a process to deepen the family's ability to catechize effectively.

The Parish

The parish is constantly catechizing by its life, worship, actions, and service. Vibrant parishes nourish adolescent catechesis. Young people, who need to experience a sense of belonging to the parish community, must be integrated into the life, mission, and work of the Church for they bring important gifts and talents to the faith community. Often times this sense of belonging and involvement in mission is created in smaller communities of adults and youth. Through this active engagement, adolescents' faith matures and their Catholic Christian identity deepens. Meaningful involvement of the "Young Church of Today" lays the foundations for the adult church of tomorrow.

Ethnic Culture

We live in a Church which is enriched by the cultural heritages of many people. These cultural heritages have an intimate link with faith. The Church has utilized the resources of different cultures to spread and explain the message of Christ and to express this message more perfectly in the liturgy and in various aspects of the life of the faithful (cf. *Gaudium et Spes,* no. 58, at *www.vatican.va/archive/ hist_councils/ii_vatican_council/documents/vat-ii_cons_19651207_ gaudium-et-spes_en.html,* accessed October 13, 2004). The strong sense of family, tradition, community, celebration, and art/music in these cultures provides building blocks for a catechesis which speaks to the experience of youth from these cultures. However, because these young people may have one foot in their ethnic culture and one foot in the dominant culture, they experience a tension that affects their growth in personal identity, values, and beliefs. This tension presents a serious challenge to adolescent catechesis.

The reality of a multicultural Church and society requires that we develop creative catechetical approaches to youth of ethnic cultures and a multicultural catechesis for all youth. We need to become aware of the riches of ethnic cultures and introduce that awareness into our catechesis. A multicultural catechesis brings youth of different cultures together to learn from each other, to develop respect for each other, and to experience Christian community with each other. Adolescent catechesis can provide a celebration of the many cultures as signs of the bountiful creation of God. We need to bring adolescents of various ethnic groups together in proper timing, in an open and nonthreatening environment, and in a respectful manner. This can help them discover their unique riches and gifts and their commonalities and place them at the service of the entire Christian community.

A Comprehensive Ministry with Youth in Parishes and Catholic Schools

Adolescent catechesis is an integral component of a broad-based comprehensive ministry with youth in a parish or Catholic school context. "Youth Catechesis is most effective within a total youth ministry" (USCCB, *Sharing the Light of Faith*, no. 228). *A Vision of Youth Ministry* outlines the components of this broader ministry with youth: Word, prayer and worship, community life, justice and service, guidance and healing, enablement, and advocacy. Faith is fostered through the entire communal life and programs of the Catholic school and of the parish youth ministry. The establishment of this broader ministerial context is essential for effective adolescent catechesis.

In developing a comprehensive ministry with youth, parishes and Catholic high schools need to collaborate. For young people, the experience of the Catholic high school can be an intense and enriching opportunity to grow in faith. Parish personnel need to recognize this reality, affirm the Catholic high school as an important resource, and develop close communication with it.

On the other hand, the Catholic high school is not a permanent experience in the life of young people because they will graduate from the school environment. Catholic high school personnel need to recognize the parish as a permanent community and seek to develop communication and coordination with parishes. The effective cooperation of parish and Catholic high school personnel can be a powerful factor in fostering the growth in faith of young people. This maturing in faith continues beyond the high school years, and parish and school leaders need to work together in ways that promote, rather than hinder, this continuing growth in faith.

The Ministry of Adolescent Catechesis

The aim, process, and principles of the ministry of adolescent catechesis are built on the six foundational themes of adolescent catechesis.

The Aim of Adolescent Catechesis

The primary aim of adolescent catechesis is to sponsor youth toward maturity in Catholic Christian faith as a living reality. We adults guide, challenge, affirm, and encourage youth in their journey toward maturity in faith. We have two tasks: to foster in youth a communal identity as Catholic Christians and to help them develop their own personal faith identity. To accomplish the first task, we present the faith convictions and values of the Catholic Christian tradition and invite adolescents to adopt and own these values and convictions. To effect the second, we help adolescents respond to God in faith, in prayer, in values, and in behavior. The sense of belonging experienced by youth in an active Christian community supports these two tasks of adolescent catechesis (cf. John Roberto, "Faith and Adolescents: Insights from Psychology and Sociology," in *Faith Maturing: A Personal and Communal Task* [Washington, DC: NFCYM, 1985], pp. 95–122).

Young people are on a journey toward the realization of a number of characteristics of Catholic Christian maturity. A systematic, planned, and intentional adolescent catechesis addresses these characteristics by blending knowledge and understanding with skills and attitudes and by emphasizing the believing, trusting, and doing dimensions of Christian faith. The following characteristics, which need to be adapted to the social and cultural settings of the ministry, provide a guide to direct the catechetical effort in the adolescent years:

- The maturing adolescent is developing a clear personal identity and is learning how to accept one's self as lovable and loved by God and others.
- The maturing adolescent is developing a commitment to a personal faith and taking responsibility for his or her own faith life and ongoing growth as a Catholic Christian, which involves the gradual realization and response to the plan, will, and purpose of God for the world.
- The maturing adolescent is developing a mature relationship with Jesus Christ whom the adolescent has come to know in a personal way in the Scriptures and in the life and teachings of the Catholic Christian community.
- The maturing adolescent is learning the skills of critical reflection that enable one to analyze life experience, society, culture, and Church in light of the Good News of Jesus Christ.
- The maturing adolescent is developing an appreciation for the importance of the Scriptures in the Christian life and learning the skills for reading and interpreting the Scriptures.
- The maturing adolescent is developing a personal pattern of personal and communal prayer and worship and understands and appreciates the sacramental life of the Church, especially the Eucharist.
- The maturing adolescent is developing an appreciation for and knowledge of the Catholic Christian tradition, its doctrinal expression, and its applicability to life in today's complex society.
- The maturing adolescent is actively engaged in the life, mission, and work of the Catholic Christian community and in particular his or her own family, the Church of the Home.
- The maturing adolescent is developing an interiorized, principled Catholic Christian moral value system and is able to confront moral issues using principles of Catholic Christian moral decision making.
- The maturing adolescent is integrating sexuality into his or her personality in a holistic way within the context of the sexual values of the Catholic Christian community and in particular his or her own family.

- The maturing adolescent is beginning to appreciate deeper relationships and is learning the skills for developing and maintaining relationships.
- The maturing adolescent is developing a life of Christian service modeled on Jesus' life and is learning that life is enriched when one gives one's self for others.
- The maturing adolescent is realizing that Christian faith means a commitment to justice and peace at the personal, interpersonal, and social/political levels of one's life and is acquiring the tools to work for justice and peace.
- The maturing adolescent is discovering how one's spirituality can be lived out through a variety of adult lifestyles.

The Process of Adolescent Catechesis

The fundamental process of adolescent catechesis involves discovering the relationships among the Catholic Christian tradition; God's present activity in the life of the adolescent, family, community, and world; and the contemporary life experience of the adolescent. "Experience is of great importance in catechesis. Experiential learning . . . gives rise to concerns and questions, hopes and anxieties, reflections and judgments, which increase one's desire to penetrate more deeply into life's meaning" (*Sharing the Light of Faith*, no. 176d). In this process, Scripture, tradition, and the contemporary life experience of youth are honored and held in dialogue. Adolescent catechesis encourages young people "to reflect on their significant experiences and respond to God's presence there" (no. 176d). It enables young people to understand the meaning of their life experience in relation to the Christian faith. The Christian faith is a tool that helps adolescents interpret and test their experience; conversely, experience is a tool that helps them to understand the Christian faith. "Experience can also increase the intelligibility of the Christian message, by providing illustrations and examples which shed light on the truths of revelation. At the same time, experience itself should be interpreted in the light of revelation" (no. 176d).

Faith often needs to be personally held and critically appropriated. As we hand on the Catholic Christian tradition and discern the activity of God in the contemporary pluralistic and secular world and in young people's own experience, we invite them to find a vocabulary to articulate their belief, to examine it, and to own it. We invite them to think for themselves, to come to their own "faith knowing." We encourage them to critically reflect upon their own experience and to allow the wisdom of Scripture and tradition to inform and transform their lives.

Catechesis reads the signs of the times—in our cultural values, in our lifestyles, in the media, and especially music, and utilizes the positive values, questions, and crises of these signs. It challenges young people to reflect actively on the impact of these signs in their lives, and consider how the Good News relates to them. Effective catechesis is in tune with the life situations of youth—their language, lifestyles, family realities, culture, and global realities. It identifies the core meanings of the signs, symbols, and images of youth today, explores how these surface in youth's lives, and relates them to the signs, symbols, and images of the Catholic Christian tradition.

Principles for Developing Adolescent Catechesis

This paper proposes ten principles to guide the work of developing adolescent catechesis in parishes and Catholic high schools. Flowing from the foundations of adolescent catechesis, the first set of five are foundational principles that describe the key understandings that shape adolescent catechesis. The second set of five are operational principles that describe the processes for developing adolescent catechesis.

Foundational Principles

1. **Adolescent catechesis is situated within the lifelong developmental process of faith growth and of ongoing catechesis. The entire catechetical effort is committed to the continuing faith growth of the individual.**

2. **Adolescent catechesis fosters Catholic Christian faith in three dimensions: trusting, believing, and doing.**

3. **Adolescent catechesis supports and encourages the role of the family and in particular the role of the parent in the faith growth of the young person and involves the parent in formulation of an adolescent catechesis curriculum and in programs to strengthen their parenting role.**

4. Adolescent catechesis respects the unique cultural heritages of young people and builds upon the positive values found in these cultural heritages, while at the same time engaging young people in examining their culture in the light of faith and examining their faith in the light of culture.

5. Adolescent catechesis is integrated and developed within a comprehensive, multifaceted approach to ministry with youth.

Operational Principles

6. Adolescent catechesis responds to the developmental, social, and cultural needs of adolescence. Related to that, the curriculum respects the changing developmental and social characteristics of the various stages of adolescence, providing a significantly different content and approach for younger and older adolescents.

Contemporary psychological and sociological research describes adolescence in distinct life phases and provides growth characteristics for each of these life stages. These characteristics serve as a guide to the learning needs of adolescents. In developing a framework for adolescent catechesis, this paper proposes catechetical faith themes for younger adolescents (11/12–14/15) and older adolescents (14/15–18/19) that draw on the psychological and sociological research. Research has also developed an understanding of family styles and life cycles. Adolescent catechesis needs to recognize and appreciate the tasks and life issues that families may be experiencing at home. In sound households the parents or parent may be encountering their own mid-life transition as the adolescent is going through his or her transition.

Research also provides a guide for developing the content (key topics) and catechetical approach (focus) for exploring a specific faith theme. The content and approach to exploring the Jesus faith theme, for example, is developed differently for younger adolescents than it is for older adolescents. Research provides a guide for selecting the particular topics and for developing specific catechetical approaches that are in keeping with the adolescent's readiness level.

The ministry of adolescent catechesis is viewed through the prism of developmental research and the social/cultural analysis of youth today. Understanding Christian faith as a lifelong journey means that catechesis first discerns a young person's developmental journey and social/cultural situation and then designs catechetical experiences that respond to the young person's particular faith needs. Patience with the gradual progress of youth is a necessity in the ministry of adolescent catechesis.

7. **Adolescent catechesis respects the variability in maturation rates and learning needs of adolescence.**

Young people mature at varied rates. A ministry with youth recognizes the varying degrees of faith maturation in young people. Many young people are in need of evangelization experiences prior to catechesis. Such experiences are essential to foster the faith growth of adolescents.

A wide variability in maturation exists within adolescent catechesis. In adolescence as much as a four-year difference in maturation rates can be seen within the same age group. In light of this, grouping only on the basis of age or grade involves serious complications for meeting the varied learning needs of youth. However, organizing adolescent catechesis around the learning needs of younger adolescents and older adolescents helps to overcome many of the difficulties of age-grading.

Implementing approaches such as individualized learning and interest grouping also helps to overcome the limitations of age-grading. Even though this principle is easier to implement in some settings than in others, we need to develop creative approaches in all settings to respect the variability in maturation and the learning needs of adolescents.

8. **Adolescent catechesis respects the expanding freedom and autonomy of adolescents.**

Adolescent catechesis is open to dialogue, question, and searching on the part of young people. It recognizes and respects the essential freedom of young people to question, doubt, rebut, and perhaps even temporarily reject the Catholic Christian faith. Catechesis must avoid coercion and manipulation.

In light of the faith readiness, learning needs, and expanding freedom and autonomy of young people, we need a variety of catechetical themes and forms of participation in adolescent catechesis. Parents and catechetical leaders can invite, encourage, and guide participation. But gradually the responsibility for participation in catechesis shifts from the family or adult authorities to the adolescent. While we can legitimately expect participation on the part of

young people, we cannot manipulate or coerce a particular faith response. With adult guidance, adolescents can select meaningful
faith themes that respond to their learning needs and the form of
their participation in catechesis. In light of this, adolescent catechesis must be attractive, interesting, creative, and responsive to the
adolescents' learning needs and must offer a variety of faith themes,
learning formats, environments, schedules, and educational techniques to encourage participation.

The principle needs to be creatively implemented in response
to the unique settings of the parish and Catholic high school.

**9. Adolescent catechesis uses a variety of learning formats,
environments, schedules, and educational techniques.**

The varied learning needs, expanding freedom, and social /
cultural situation of adolescents suggest that catechetical planners
offer a variety of learning formats, environments, schedules, and
techniques. In developing catechetical programming, planners can
draw upon various learning formats (mini-courses, seasonal programming such as Advent and Lent, small-group learning teams, youth
fellowship, intergenerational programming, worship / celebration,
action learning, retreats, study tours / trips, individualized learning,
and peer ministry) and various scheduling options (weekly, bi-week-
ly, full day, monthly, overnight, weekend, and week-long). Our selection of formats, environments, schedules, and techniques needs
to fit local needs, circumstances, and resources.

Catholic schools have much experience in providing a variety
of schedules and formats for responding to the differing abilities,
needs, and interests of students. This experience can be a rich resource in designing a flexible and creative approach to the structure
and scheduling of the catechetical program and curriculum. Core
topics and electives presented in a variety of formats, such as long-
and short-term courses, independent study, retreats, and service involvement, can provide a creative and flexible way to weave the
various faith themes into the catechetical program of the school. In
this way we can develop a comprehensive response to the varying
maturation rates and the expanding freedom and autonomy of the
students.

The particular needs of parish adolescent catechesis suggest
short-term, rather than long-term, programming. Young people
have increased demands placed upon their time. Catechesis adapts

to their world by offering a diversity of faith themes in a variety of short-term formats. Short-term learning opportunities actually increase the participation of youth and encourage them to engage in multiple learning experiences throughout the year.

10. **Adolescent catechesis best responds to the learning needs of adolescents when it is focused on particular faith themes.**

A thematic approach to catechesis for younger and older adolescents draws faith themes from the Catholic Christian tradition and the developmental, sociological, and cultural research on youth. It focuses the exploration of a faith theme on selected topics (content) that provide possibilities for exploring the theme in some depth. Instead of surveying the broad scope of a particular faith theme, this approach selects a primary focus and key topics in keeping with the adolescent's developmental and social readiness. In the context of lifelong learning, these faith themes for young and older adolescents have been selected because of their particular importance at this stage of a person's life. This approach to adolescent catechesis builds on the foundations developed in childhood catechesis and looks to young adult and adult catechesis for continued opportunities for learning.

A Framework for Adolescent Catechesis

An Integrated Catechesis

By focusing on key faith themes, adolescent catechesis provides a systematic, orderly, and focused presentation of the Catholic Christian tradition. Six integral dimensions are woven throughout each of these themes.

Jesus Christ. Every faith theme includes a discussion of its relationship to Jesus and the Gospel. Thus the adolescent develops an understanding of Jesus and his message and is invited to a personal response in faith to both.

Scripture. The catechesis for each faith theme is grounded in Scripture. This fosters in adolescents a deepening knowledge and appreciation of the Scriptures in the Church's tradition and in their own lives.

Church. Each faith theme affirms the vision of the Church as a historical community of people committed to the vision, values, and mission of Jesus. In seeking to create experiences of such a community, ministers establish this Church in the minds and hearts of the young people.

Prayer. Each faith theme leads to and flows from prayer. Adolescents learn to pray by personally and communally experiencing prayer.

Action/lifestyle. Each faith theme leads to action that reflects a Christian lifestyle. This empowers young people to live a more faithful Christian life—personally, interpersonally, and socially / politically.

Interpretation and critical reflection. Each faith theme seeks to promote critical reflection and interpretation that affirms and critiques the values and behaviors of culture and society. This enables young people to interpret their own culture, ethnic culture, society, and life experience in light of the Catholic Christian faith.

Introduction to the Framework

This framework presents faith themes designed in light of the learning needs of younger adolescents and older adolescents. The framework, which can be used as the basis for developing the scope, sequence, and objectives of a curriculum, is not intended to serve all the needs of a given situation. Local leaders need to adapt the framework to the particular needs of their youth, and they may also need to include additional faith themes not presented in this paper.

The suggested content for the faith themes is drawn from the Catholic Christian tradition and the developmental, sociological, and cultural research on youth. The selection of each faith theme is designed to "shed the light of the Christian message on the realities which have greater impact on the adolescent" (*General Catechetical Directory*, no. 84). The catechetical focus for each faith theme is in keeping with the developmental and social readiness of the adolescent. Themes that occur for both younger and older adolescents are given new perspectives in light of the adolescent's experience.

Faith Themes for Younger Adolescents (11/12–14/15)

Church

Focus: This faith theme helps younger adolescents understand and experience the Catholic Christian story and mission and become involved in the Christian community.

Suggested Content:
- the story of the Church as related to the younger adolescent's story;
- Jesus' mission and ministry as these continue today through the Christian community's ministries of Word, worship, community building, and service;
- the global and multicultural reality of the Church;
- the community life and ministries in the other major Christian churches;
- involvement in the life, mission, and work of the parish community and the family.

Jesus and the Gospel Message

Focus: This faith theme helps younger adolescents follow Jesus, develop a more personal relationship with Him, concentrate on the person and teaching of Jesus, discover what a relationship with Jesus means, and respond to Jesus from a growing inner sense of self.

Suggested Content:
- Christian faith as a personal response to and relationship with Jesus;
- Gospel discipleship or the exploring of what following Jesus and living the Good News means;
- the person of Jesus—his values, intentions, motives, and attitudes;
- the key themes of the Good News (what Jesus teaches us about God, prayer, justice/peace, service, and moral life);

- the impact of the Good News on the adolescent's life;
- the response of the first disciples to Jesus and the Good News

Morality and Moral Decision Making

Focus: This faith theme helps younger adolescents apply Catholic Christian moral values as maturing persons who are becoming increasingly capable of using decision-making skills to make free and responsible choices.

Suggested Content:
- Jesus' vision of being fully human as the foundation of Catholic Christian morality;
- the moral values in Jesus' teachings;
- Catholic Christian moral values that relate to the life of the adolescent;
- the basis of moral decision making within a Catholic Christian context: conscience, sin, and reconciliation;
- four sources of moral maturing: mind, heart, family / other persons, and Catholic Christian tradition;
- skills for critically reflecting on self, youth culture, and media and society's values in light of Catholic Christian moral values.

Personal Growth

Focus: This faith theme helps younger adolescents develop a stronger and more realistic concept of self by exploring who they are and who they can become.

Suggested Content:
- the building of a strong and realistic concept of self with an emphasis on self-concept, growing autonomy, and self-determination;
- Jesus' vision of being fully human and its impact on the younger adolescent's growing identity as a Christian;
- the response of the Good News and tradition to adolescent struggles (isolation, loneliness, frustration, anger) and problems (suicide, substance abuse);
- the development of skills for handling peer pressure and values, and adolescent problems.

Relationships

Focus: This faith theme helps younger adolescents develop more mutual, trusting, and loyal relationships with peers, parents, and other adults by emphasizing skills that enhance and maintain relationships.

Suggested Content:
- the nature of relationships;
- Jesus' life of service and teaching on living a life of loving service;
- relationships in the Christian community;
- the development of responsible relationships with an emphasis on honesty, love, and respect;
- the development of skills, such as active listening and self-disclosure, for communicating with peers, parents, and other adults.

Service

Focus: This faith theme helps younger adolescents explore Jesus' call to live a life of loving service, discover that such a life is integral to discipleship, develop a foundation for a social justice consciousness, and participate in service that involves relationships and concrete action.

Suggested Content:
- Jesus' life of service and his teaching on living a life of loving service;
- service as an essential element of discipleship;
- the development of knowledge and skills needed to engage in service;
- service projects;
- reflection on involvement in service projects.

Sexuality

Focus: This faith theme helps younger adolescents learn about sexual development, better understand the dynamics of maturing as a sexual person within a Catholic Christian's value context, and discuss sexuality with their parents using a Catholic Christian value-based approach.

Suggested Content:
- sexual development with an emphasis on accurate information;
- sexuality as integral to one's personal identity with an explanation of gender identity and roles;
- relationships and dating;
- Catholic Christian understanding of sexuality and sexual moral values.

Faith Themes for Older Adolescents (14/15–18/19)

Faith and Identity

Focus: This faith theme helps older adolescents explore what being a Christian, a Catholic, and a person of faith means; appraise the faith of the community; develop their own personally-held faith and own it; and grow in response to the Gospel challenge to be a person of faith.

Suggested Content:
- the meaning and experience of revelation and of God's actions in our lives;
- faith as a gift, as a process of understanding the basic questions that all persons face as a dynamic and positive force that can shape the adolescent's life and personality and ongoing process of conversion;
- reflection on present faith growth and struggles;
- the development of skills for reflection;
- Jesus as the model of a completely faithful person;
- Catholic Christian beliefs with an emphasis on integrating these beliefs into a personal identity;
- the beliefs and faith traditions of the major Christian churches—their uniqueness and what they share in common with the Catholic Christian church.

The Gospels

Focus: This faith theme helps older adolescents appreciate the historical and literary development, structure, and major themes of the four Gospels; grasp insights that come from scriptural scholarship; and utilize these insights to interpret the Gospels.

Suggested Content:

- the three stages of Gospel development;
- revelation and inspiration;
- a study of the writing styles of the Evangelists and the structure of the Gospels;
- an in-depth exploration of one particular Synoptic Gospel.

Hebrew Scriptures

Focus: This faith theme helps older adolescents appreciate the historical and literary development, structure, and major themes of the Hebrew Scriptures, grasp the insights that come from scriptural scholarship; and utilize these insights in interpreting the Scriptures.

Suggested Content:

- the growth, composition, historical development, writing styles and methods, and structure of the Hebrew Scriptures;
- revelation, inspiration, and biblical interpretation;
- the reading and interpreting of the Hebrew Scriptures;
- exploration of the major themes and life questions of the Hebrew Scriptures and their relevance to today.

Jesus

Focus: This faith theme helps older adolescents explore who Jesus Christ is, discover his meaning for their lives, and develop a personal, deeply relational experience of Him.

Suggested Content:

- the historical and social world of Jesus;
- Jesus' relationship with his Father and his image of God;
- Jesus' life, mission, and the key themes of his message;
- Jesus' death, resurrection, and ongoing presence;
- the Spirit and the Church throughout history;
- new ways of thinking about Jesus today;
- ways to develop a richer, more mature relationship with Jesus.

Justice and Peace

Focus: This faith theme helps older adolescents develop a global social consciousness and compassion grounded in the Christian vision and attentive to the needs of those who are hurting and who are oppressed.

Suggested Content:
- the Scriptural vision of life (justice, peace, equality, and steward-ship);
- the call to conversion, to live the vision, values, and lifestyle of the reign of God;
- an analysis of the social problems and injustices in the world, such as hunger, poverty, war/peace, inequality, discrimination, and ecology;
- the determination of a constructive, Christian response to these problems on the personal, interpersonal, and social/political levels of one's life;
- the development of practical skills such as peaceful conflict resolution and organization for action;
- the recognition of the injustices experienced by young people themselves.

Love and Lifestyles

Focus: This faith theme helps older adolescents explore their maturing and sexual identity; use skills for developing intimate, trusting, enduring relationships; and discover how their spirituality can be lived out through a variety of lifestyles.

Suggested Content:
- Christian view of sexuality and intimacy;
- how to build love relationships and develop intimacy;
- dating;
- development of a sexual identity;
- how single persons, priests, deacons, vowed religious, and married persons live as Christians;
- the choice of a lifestyle;
- the improvements of life decision-making skills;
- Christian marriage, love, and family life in today's world.

Morality

Focus: This faith theme helps older adolescents critique their personal and social values; develop and use an interiorized, principled moral value system; and understand the role of Christian conscience and moral decision making in the development of this interiorized moral value system.

Suggested Content:

- the development of an adult conscience based on Catholic Christian moral principles with emphasis on taking responsibility for one's moral values, actions, and lifestyles;
- how to interiorize a personally chosen set of moral principles and values;
- the confrontation and resolution of moral dilemmas;
- the development of skills for critically reflecting on self, youth culture, and media and society's values in the light of Catholic Christian moral values.

Paul and His Letters

Focus: This faith theme helps older adolescents develop an understanding of the historical context, literary style, and major themes of Paul's Letters; utilize the insights of scriptural scholarship to interpret his writings; and discover Paul as apostle, preacher, theologian, and man of faith.

Suggested Content:

- the early church communities as the context and setting for Paul's letters;
- Paul's missionary journeys, sufferings, and trials;
- the major practical and pastoral problems to which Paul responded;
- the major theological themes of Paul's Letters as seen especially in his letters to the Galatians and Romans.

Prayer and Worship

Focus: This faith theme helps older adolescents develop a personally-held spirituality and a rich personal and communal prayer life.

Suggested Content:

- the nature of prayer;
- Jesus as a person of prayer;
- Jesus' teachings on prayer;
- an exploration of images and concepts of God;
- the development of a personal prayer life by exploring the who, what, when, where, why, and how of prayer and by experimenting with and experiencing a variety of prayer forms and styles;

- the Church's worship and sacramental life;
- an experience of the richness of the community's communal prayer.

Adolescent Catechesis and Confirmation

There is much diversity in the age and practice of Confirmation in the United States. When Confirmation is celebrated in the adolescent years, it affords the parish a significant opportunity to foster the faith maturing of adolescents. This paper offers a catechetical context within which to view Confirmation preparation. The aim, process, and principles proposed in "The Ministry of Adolescent Catechesis" directly apply to the practice of Confirmation. Confirmation catechesis needs to embody the process articulated by this paper. The ten principles developed in this paper are a guide to the development of the preparation process for Confirmation. Realizing that sacramental preparation for Confirmation has a distinct catechesis with its own focus and elements, this paper does not address that specific catechesis. It does propose that the fully initiated Christian is not the fully mature Christian. Catechesis is lifelong and the Christian community needs to provide learning opportunities for continuing growth in faith. Therefore, the faith themes presented in this paper can serve as a foundation prior to Confirmation catechesis and as a continuing catechesis after the celebration of the sacrament.

Leaders in the Ministry of Adolescent Catechesis

The collaborative ministry of adolescent catechesis requires the integration of a variety of leaders with specialized roles. The effectiveness of adolescent catechesis relies on the contribution of all leaders. In "The Foundations of Adolescent Catechesis," this paper identified the important contributions that the family, in particular parents, and the parish community make to the faith maturing of adolescents. The parent is the primary educator. However, the roles identified in this section complement and support the parent's role. This section examines the specific roles and responsibilities of catechists / religion teachers and of coordinators of adolescent catechesis in parish, school, and diocesan settings.

Catechists / Religion Teachers

Catechists / religion teachers hold a central role within the ministry of adolescent catechesis, second only to the parents. They are formally involved in an actual learning setting with youth, sponsoring them in their journey to maturity in Catholic Christian faith. The role of catechist in a parish setting may be exercised by both pastoral leaders (priest, DRE, coordinator of youth ministry) and designated members of the Christian community. The Church calls catechists / religion teachers to work toward developing the following competencies, recognizing that growth as a catechists / religion teacher is an ongoing process.

Qualities of Catechists / Religion Teachers

Catechists / religion teachers are first and foremost **Persons of Faith** with a vibrant personal relationship with Jesus and a well-developed life of prayer. They recognize that they are called to exercise their gifts in catechetical ministry. Catechists / religion teachers are **Witnesses of the Gospel** who believe and live the Good News of Jesus within the Catholic Christian tradition and want to share that faith with others. They witness to the Good News in their life and teaching ministry. Catechists / religion teachers are **Witnesses of the Church**, committed to the Catholic Church and the Church's teaching mission. They are **Sharers in the Fellowship of the Spirit**, participating in the ongoing communal life of the parish, developing a spirit of community with other catechists, and dealing with conflict and disagreement in a sensitive and understanding manner. Catechists / religion teachers are **Servants of the Community**, responding to the needs of individuals and community. Catechists / religion teachers are **knowledgeable of the Catholic Christian tradition** and have a fundamental understanding of the scriptural, doctrinal, and moral expression of the Catholic faith. In addition, they are committed to continued growth as Catholic Christians and as catechists / religion teachers (cf. *Sharing the Light of Faith,* nos. 205–211).

Above and beyond these qualities, catechists / religion teachers possess a genuine love for young people and display qualities that demonstrate this love: **availability, acceptance, authenticity, and vulnerability.** An encounter with an adolescent requires an openness, a presence, and real availability. Adolescents need to know that they are welcome to come and talk on their own terms. Catechists / religion teachers understand the questions, struggles, and concerns of youth and appreciate them for who they are—persons loved by God. These adolescents seek out Catechists / religion teachers who can authentically share their own faith story—the struggles, hopes, and doubts that they experience in their own lives. By this interaction with adolescents, catechists / religion teachers quietly demonstrate an inner acceptance of the adolescents' journey for personal meaning. Catechists / religion teachers who are capable of being vulnerable provide a tremendous support to the adolescent, encouraging the adolescent's growth toward maturity as an adult. When the adolescent perceives a catechist / religion teacher who is comfortable with personal limitations and capable of admitting failure, the way is opened for the adolescent's own personal self-acceptance (cf. Charles M. Shelton, *Adolescent Spirituality: Pastoral Ministry for High School and College Youth* [Chicago: Loyola University Press, 1983], pp. 320–342).

Education of Catechists / Religion Teachers

"Because catechists approach their task with varying degrees of competence, programs should be designed to help individuals acquire the particular knowledge and skills they need" (*Sharing the Light of Faith,* no. 213). The entire Church through diocesan offices, parishes, schools, universities, formation centers, etc., needs to provide education for catechists / religion teachers. This education focuses on the spiritual and theological growth of the person and the development of understandings and skills necessary for adolescent catechesis.

Spirituality of the Catechist / Religion Teacher

The catechist / religion teacher demonstrates the following qualities:

• a willingness and ability to speak with conviction about his or her own experience and convictions as a Catholic Christian;

- continuing growth in his or her personal and communal prayer life;
- an ability to see God's activity in his or her experience, ministry, and lifestyle.

Knowledge of the Adolescent

The catechist / religion teacher demonstrates a fundamental understanding of the following:

- the characteristics of adolescent growth and development drawn from psychology, moral and faith development, sociology, and research on family life cycle, family systems, the socio-economic situation of the family, and how these relate to catechetical ministry with youth;
- the characteristics and values of our society, of youth culture, of ethnic culture, of media/music, etc., and their impact on the life of the adolescent and how it relates to catechetical ministry with youth;
- the signs, symbols, images, language, and culture of youth and how these surface in youth's lives and how these relate to catechetical ministry with youth.

Skills for Adolescent Catechesis

The catechist / religion teacher demonstrates the ability to do the following:

- design and conduct learning experiences for youth, utilizing a variety of learning processes, media, methods, and resources;
- relate the Gospel to the world of youth in the language, signs, symbols, and images understandable to youth;
- utilize communication, group discussion, community building, faith-sharing, and storytelling processes and skills;
- design and conduct worship, prayer, justice, and service experiences with youth.

Content of Catechesis

The catechist / religion teacher demonstrates a fundamental understanding of the following content:

- the development and key themes of the Hebrew and Christian Scriptures and the way to utilize the tools of scriptural scholarship to interpret the Scriptures for his or her life;

- Jesus Christ (his life, mission, message, death, and resurrection) and the historical development and contemporary approach to the Church's understanding of Jesus;
- the models of the Church as mystery, people of God, faith community, mystical body, and institution, and the Church's mission and ministries in today's world, a global, multicultural Church;
- contemporary sacramental theology and the role of the sacraments within the Christian life;
- Catholic Christian morality, conscience, personal and social sin, and moral decision making;
- the development and major themes of the Church's teachings on justice and peace and how they relate to our world;
- the core beliefs/doctrines (e.g., Trinity, Salvation, Grace) of Catholic Christianity and their expression within the contemporary Church.

Coordinators of Adolescent Catechesis in a Parish Setting

The following brief descriptions of the coordinators in parish settings is offered as a means for clarifying the variety of coordination roles in adolescent catechesis. Each of these coordinators needs a thorough understanding of the adolescent and of the aims, processes, and principles of adolescent catechesis. Those coordinators directly responsible for adolescent catechesis need the qualities, knowledge, and skills of the catechist.

Coordinator of Youth Ministry

The primary task of the coordinator of youth ministry (CYM) is to facilitate the harmonious working together of the various personnel and programs that embody the parish youth ministry efforts. These programs serve to develop a comprehensive ministry embracing Word, worship, community life, justice / service, guidance / healing, enablement, and advocacy. An integral dimension of this comprehensive ministry is catechesis. The harmonious functioning of a youth ministry requires the involvement of the CYM in adolescent catechesis.

Directors of Religious Education

The primary task of the director of religious education (DRE) is to facilitate the development of personnel and programs for lifelong catechesis in the parish. These programs span each age group from childhood catechesis through adolescent and adult catechesis. In addition the DRE is often responsible for sacramental preparation and is often involved in the adult catechumenate (RCIA). The integration of a lifelong catechesis requires the involvement of the DRE in adolescent catechesis (cf. *Sharing the Light of Faith,* no. 214).

Priests / Pastoral Associates

Priests / pastoral associates often exercise the role of CYM or DRE. They also "exercise a uniquely important role and have a special responsibility for the success of the catechetical ministry. They are a source of leadership, cooperation, and support for all involved in this ministry" (*Sharing the Light of Faith,* no. 217). Through preaching, liturgical-sacramental ministry, and presence to young people, the priest and pastoral minister play a central factor in adolescent catechesis (cf. no. 217). Among the parish leaders, the pastor is "primarily responsible for seeing to it that the catechetical needs, goals, and priorities of the parish are identified, articulated and met" (no. 217). A collaborative approach is needed to harmonize the role of priests / pastoral associates with the DRE and CYM.

A Collaborative Approach

Adolescent catechesis represents the intersection of the responsibility of the CYM or DRE. The DRE is responsible for catechesis throughout the lifespan. The CYM is responsible for a specific age group. The CYM brings the perspective of a comprehensive ministry to a wide set of youth needs and understands the integral place of catechesis within this ministry. The DRE brings the perspective of a lifelong approach to catechesis and understands the integral place of adolescent catechesis within this lifelong approach. From this perspective, both the DRE and CYM share responsibility for the adolescent catechesis program. This situation may cause tension that needs to be worked through. The clarification of responsibility for adolescent catechesis is based on the education, competence, and experience of the people involved in catechesis and ministry with youth. Using the four functions outlined below, leaders can clarify the exact nature of that shared responsibility.

Collaboration and teamwork are requirements for effective adolescent catechesis.

An essential ingredient in a collaborative approach is the involvement of parents and families in adolescent catechesis. Coordinators of adolescent catechesis in parish settings need to listen to
families, involve parents and families in planning for adolescent
catechesis, articulate what is happening with the families of the
parish, and build in a family perspective within adolescent catechesis.

Clarifying Roles—Four Functions

Each of the above leadership roles (the coordinator of youth
ministry, the director of religious education, and the priest / pastoral
associate) are involved in the parish catechetical effort. The parish
can use the following four functions to discuss and clarify the responsibilities of the CYM, DRE, and priest / pastoral associate in
adolescent catechesis. Determining the pattern of relationships and
responsibilities among these leaders is critically important. This
clarification demands collaboration and teamwork by the CYM,
DRE, and priest / pastoral associate. Through this process of clarification, a person(s) can be designated to develop and coordinate
adolescent catechesis.

The **Advocate** works to educate the appropriate leadership
about adolescent catechesis, about the needs of young people and
their families, and about processes and programs that can be developed to meet these needs. The Advocate does not assume direct
responsibility for developing programs but, rather, indicates continued growth possibilities. The **Resource Person** helps those involved in adolescent catechesis to become aware of diocesan
services, newly published print and audio-visual materials, workshops, training programs, and conferences. The Resource Person
keeps abreast of new resources and channels the information to
other leaders. The **Coordinator** assumes organizational direction
for the adolescent catechesis program, developing the program with
a planning team, recruiting/training/supporting catechists, and ad-
ministering the program. The **Catechist** is directly involved in designing and conducting learning experiences with youth.

Coordinators of Adolescent Catechesis in a Catholic School Setting

School Principals

As the primary administrator and coordinator of the school's ministry, the principal is primarily responsible for seeing to it that the catechetical needs, goals, and priorities of the school are identified, articulated, and met. He or she facilitates the development of a shared philosophy and shared planning among the administrators and faculty to build a faith community in the school and to provide for a holistic ministry with the students. The principal also provides opportunities for the ongoing education of faculty members by which they can deepen their faith and enhance their ministry with youth (cf. *Sharing the Light of Faith*, no. 215).

High School Campus Ministry Coordinator

The primary task of the high school campus ministry coordinator is to call forth the ministerial talents of those in the school community to help organize, motivate, and initiate a coordinated and holistic ministry at the high school level. This often involves a complex of programs and activities in each of the components of youth ministry: Word, worship, community life, justice/service, guidance/healing, enablement, and advocacy. All of these are aimed at building a living faith community among students, faculty, and administration. The high school campus ministry coordinator works with the religious studies department, the chaplain, and the guidance department to create an environment in which their respective programs are experienced by the students as complementary. The harmonious functioning of a high school campus ministry requires the collaboration of the coordinator with the religious studies department, the chaplain, and the guidance department. In addition, it is essential for the high school campus minister to be in close collaboration with parish youth ministry efforts.

Religious Studies Department Chairperson

The primary task of the department chairperson is to facilitate the development of curricula and personnel for catechesis in the high school. In addition to his or her responsibilities as a religion teacher, the chairperson shares responsibility for coordinating the ministry of catechesis within the school community. He or she often assumes the roles of advocate and resource person, in addition to those of religion teacher and coordinator. As one dimension of a broader ministry within the school, the chairperson collaborates with the coordinator of campus ministry, the chaplain, and the guidance department to provide an integrated, total ministry.

Adolescent Catechesis in the Diocesan Church

Diocesan Offices

Diocesan offices of religious education, youth ministry, and Catholic schools are catalysts for the vision and development of adolescent catechesis within the diocese. Through their training, consultation, and resourcing services they assist parishes and schools in the development of adolescent catechesis programs. These indirect services focus on the key leaders who have the responsibility for adolescent catechesis in parishes and schools. These diocesan offices must collaborate in formulating and implementing a plan for educating parish and school leaders to the foundations, aims, process, principles, and framework of adolescent catechesis contained in this paper. A collaborative effort is also needed in providing curriculum development assistance to parishes and schools, in making available current resources for adolescent catechesis, and in providing education programs for catechists / religion teachers. Special attention needs to be given to assisting parishes and schools in developing multicultural and multiracial catechetical programming, to making available multicultural and multiracial catechetical resources, and to educating coordinators and catechists / religion teachers on the educational methods and techniques suited to the cultural, racial, and linguistic needs of the people in the diocese. Consultation services to assist parishes and Catholic schools in clarifying responsibility for adolescent catechesis may also be required (cf. *Sharing the Light of Faith*, no. 238).

Bishops

The urgency of the present situation of adolescent catechesis necessitates the active encouragement and support of the bishop for new initiatives in adolescent catechesis. His active involvement through support of diocesan and local efforts, through his pastoral visits, and through his communication in pastoral letters and the media brings the Church's concern for adolescent catechesis to the forefront. As chief catechist in the diocese, he is "responsible for seeing to it that sound catechesis is provided for all people" (*Sharing the Light of Faith*, no. 218). The active support and involvement of the bishop is essential for helping all ecclesial communities realize that youth are more than the church of the future—they are the "Young Church of Today."

Conclusion

The content of this paper and the extensive consultation process through which it was prepared speak strongly about the need for, elements of, and principles for developing adolescent catechesis. However, this paper is not the final word. If the paper has validity, it will best be seen in effective implementation of adolescent catechesis in families, parishes, schools, diocesan programs, and national efforts. Readers of this paper are urged to reflect on the paper, react to it, criticize it, and use it in assessing current efforts in adolescent catechesis and in designing and implementing new and/or renewed efforts.

In striving to enrich and affirm the life and faith of young people through catechesis, it is humbling to realize that our best efforts may not always bring forth the fruit that was intended or hoped for. "It [catechesis] is more difficult and tiring than ever before, because of the obstacles and difficulties of all kinds that it meets" (*Catechesis in Our Time*, no. 40). However, this should not cause us discouragement or laxity. Youth deserve our very best efforts, even if we do not often see the fruits of our efforts. Yet in the long run, we all must rely on the presence and power of the Spirit of God. Adults and youth are challenged to be open to the urging and movement of the Holy Spirit in the process of catechesis. Pope John Paul II has described this reality well. This paper concludes with his words. This is also the point where the next words and steps belong to us.

> Catechesis, which is growth in faith and the maturing of the Christian life toward its fullness, is consequently a work of the Holy Spirit, a work that the Spirit alone can initiate and sustain in the Church. (*Catechesis in Our Time*, no. 72)

Chapter 4

The Challenge of Catholic Youth Evangelization: Called to Be Witnesses and Storytellers

The Challenge
of Catholic Youth Evangelization

Preamble

This document builds on the rich tradition in youth ministry begun with *A Vision of Youth Ministry,* published in 1986, and furthered by the publication of *The Challenge of Adolescent Catechesis,* in 1986 (Washington, DC: National Federation for Catholic Youth Ministry). Just as recognized needs were responded to by those documents, so too recent experiences in ministry with adolescents have given rise to new challenges concerning the Gospel mandate to proclaim effectively and pass on the Good News to the adolescents of today. One new challenge, and the focus of this document, is the great need to clarify the meaning, content, principles, and methods of the effective evangelization of young people.

Within the Church, there has been considerable growth in our understanding of evangelization, and Catholics are reclaiming this ministry as part of our rich tradition. However, for some Catholics today, evangelization still causes anxiety. The term elicits a wide range of reactions, from fear of fundamentalism to past and often negative presumptions about missionary work. The ministry of evangelization might prompt stereotypical images of rather aggressive Christians trying to recruit new church members through proselytizing, door knocking and public faith-witnessing.

Even as more and more Catholics understand that they are called to represent the church and are being equipped to do so, many are still uncertain if they have the background and knowledge of doctrine deemed necessary to represent the church to others. Discomfort with areas of Church teaching and practice might cause some to be reluctant to share their faith convictions with others. All of these concerns are the result of an incomplete, if not inaccurate, understanding of evangelization.

The Roman Catholic Church's history of evangelizing efforts may also contribute to our current anxiety about this ministry. There have been times when a lack of respect for human dignity, coupled with an oppressive colonization, resulted in the subjugation and even destruction of a people's culture, often in the name of evangelization. We have to acknowledge such failures in our history and reconcile with those whom we have neglected or continue to marginalize, even as we now move towards a more inclusive, sensitive and Gospel-based approach to evangelization.

The anxieties, discomforts and past failures underscore the importance of articulating clearly a contemporary understanding of evangelization. The Roman Catholic Church is a community with certain beliefs, practices, and traditions that is challenged to speak the transforming word of God to all societies and cultures. Out of our history a particular style of Catholic evangelization is emerging, and in this document we will more fully articulate and describe this understanding for the benefit of our ministry with young people.

Each generation, as well as each individual, has the challenge of addressing the ultimate questions of personal meaning and purpose in life and the response of faith to both. The young people who come to maturity today have a similar task and responsibility. A thorough social analysis of the contemporary world of youth would describe the modern pressures and issues that many say are unique to the current generation of adolescents, which only add to the challenge of addressing their questions regarding faith and religion. Our ministry efforts in enabling young people to confront their important questions and issues have had mixed results.

- Why are some of our efforts in youth ministry exciting and effective, while others seem boring and lifeless?
- Why do some young people grow to a mature and knowledgeable faith, while others, despite our best efforts in adolescent catechesis, see faith as irrelevant?
- Why do so many young Catholics leave the Church for other faith communities?
- Why are some experiences of liturgy alive and celebratory for young people, while others seem like meaningless and empty ritual?
- How can we make confirmation an initiation into full faith life, rather than the sacrament of graduation out of the Church?
- Why do some young people experience crises as opportunities for growth, while others seem to self-destruct when life becomes difficult?
- Why do some children seem to abandon the faith journey even when parents do everything "right"?

- How can we instill in young people the values of compassion and justice in the midst of a society that lauds individualism and consumerism?

Most people involved in youth ministry will identify with one or more of these questions. We are challenged to identify the ingredient that truly energizes our ministry, if we are to enable young people to grow to a mature Gospel faith. It is the contention of this document that the ingredient is evangelization.

Perhaps the signs of our times echo the situation confronting Jesus: "When he saw the crowds, he had compassion for them, because they were harassed and helpless, like sheep without a shepherd. Then he said to his disciples, 'The harvest is plentiful, but the laborers are few; therefore ask the Lord of the harvest to send out laborers into his harvest'" (Matt. 9:36–38).

The impetus for a new understanding of evangelization, especially as integrated into our understanding of youth ministry, comes from the Gospel of John: "Do you not say, 'Four months more, then comes the harvest'? But I tell you, look around you, and see how the fields are ripe for harvesting" (4:35). Catholic youth ministry is challenged to accept fully the task of evangelization.

Definition

As we seek a definition of evangelization, we look to Luke's account of Jesus in the synagogue, quoting Isaiah:

"The Spirit of the Lord is upon me,
because he has anointed me
to bring good news to the poor.
He has sent me to proclaim release to the captives
and recovery of sight to the blind,
to let the oppressed go free,
to proclaim the year of the Lord's favor."

(Luke 4:18–19)

Jesus then proclaims, "Today this scripture has been fulfilled in your hearing" (Luke 4:21). He says that the reign of God has arrived in himself.

Drawing from Jesus' example, evangelization involves the community's pronouncement and living witness that the reign of God has become realized in and through Jesus. As evangelizers, as heralds of good news, our task is to share the Good News of the reign of God and to invite young people to hear about the Word Made Flesh.

In attempting to develop a working definition of evangelization, we must take to heart a caution expressed by Pope Paul VI in his apostolic exhortation on evangelization, *Evangelii Nuntiandi:*

> Any partial and fragmentary definition which attempts to render the reality of evangelization in all its richness, complexity and dynamism does so only at the risk of impoverishing it and even of distorting it. It is impossible to grasp the concept of evangelization unless one tries to keep in view all its essential elements. (No. 17)

With this caution in mind, for the purposes of this document, evangelization has two fundamental meanings:

- First of all, evangelism is the **initial** effort by the faith community as a whole to proclaim through word and witness the Good News of the Gospel to those who have not yet heard or seen it, and then to invite those persons into a relationship with Jesus Christ and the community of believers.
- Second, evangelization is the **ongoing** witness of the faith community as it attempts to live out the Gospel with such authenticity that the faith of all the members is sustained and nourished. As such, evangelization is recognized as the energizing core of the life of the Church and all its ministries: word, sacrament, all forms of pastoral ministry, and justice and service.

Evangelization, it should be emphasized, is directed not only towards members of the church. The community's witness is also to the larger culture, society, and world with a goal to transform humanity. The Catholic Church has been very clear that evangelization must be concerned not only with the personal conversion of its members but also with the conversion of the wider culture (cf. *Evangelii Nuntiandi*, no. 20).

Goal of This Document

In presenting our understanding of the effective evangelization of young people, this document strives to be descriptive and prophetic, rather than programmatic. This document will articulate a vision for Catholic youth evangelization by identifying the foundations, principles, and dynamics of effective evangelization, as well as by describing the integration of evangelization into comprehensive youth ministry.

This document is intended to prompt further reflection and discussion and is not meant to be the final word on youth evangelization. Rather than attempt specific applications to various ministry settings, our hope is to provide a clearer focus and direction for our efforts in evangelization and to invite the entire community into a continuing dialogue about this vital dimension of our ministry with young people.

Audience

This document is addressed to the entire faith community, but specifically to leaders in ministry to young people in parish, school, community, and diocesan settings, and to leaders in related faith-formation ministries. It will also be of interest to many others who now serve young people: family ministry staffs, youth retreat program directors, justice ministry workers, scouting leaders, athletic directors, youth club staffs, ministers to persons with disabilities, and youth-serving organizations and movements.

Foundations of Catholic Youth Evangelization

As reflected in *A Vision of Youth Ministry,* particularly in its use of the Emmaus story (see Luke 24:13–35) as a model of effective ministry, ministry with young people must be similar to the ministry of Jesus. An understanding of Jesus' ministry and its applicability to the situation of young people today provides the foundation for effective Catholic youth evangelization.

"And the Word became flesh and lived among us" (John 1:14). Jesus is God and the fullest revelation of God, and his ways are the embodiment of God's ways in this world. Therefore, Jesus' ministry, death, and resurrection are normative for our faith and are the source of our ministry. We are challenged to place the story of Jesus into dialogue with our own ministry, and certainly with our own lives and the lives of our young people.

The Message and Ministry of Jesus

The central theme of Jesus' message and ministry was the nearness of the reign of God. This reign is made present and real whenever and wherever God is known and God's will is done. As revealed in Jesus, God calls us to intimate union, and in this union we find wholeness, healing, and salvation. Jesus proclaimed not only what God does for us, but who God is in relationship to us. The reign of God is characterized by fullness of life with God and a fullness of life for all God's people, loved unconditionally by the One who created them. Jesus announces in word and in action that the reign of God is already breaking through, that God is drawing near with salvation for all, and that the response demanded of people to the reign is to turn their lives around, repent, and believe in the Good News. This Jesus, who surprises us and seems outrageous in his proclamation, calls us to *metanoia,* that is, to conversion and acceptance of the reign of God.

Jesus did not just speak of the reign of God; he embodied it. He witnessed to the reign of God in his experience of God's nearness as "Abba." His life proclaimed the reign of God, and God's saving grace was released through Jesus for the salvation of all.

Jesus invited those who heard his message into a community of disciples who traveled with him—listening, learning, knowing, loving, watching, and then being sent forth on a mission to become the first witnesses to the presence of the reign of God in Jesus and the first to tell the story of Jesus to others.

Jesus especially reached out to the poor and the weak, to the powerless and marginalized people of his society. His ministry demonstrated the triumph of God's reign over the forces and conditions that bind and blind people. Jesus' message of the reign of God is both gift and challenge, one that demands a price of those who would accept it. Accepting the reign of God involves entering into God's love towards the oppressed. The reign of God is one of justice and peace, of compassion and hope—qualities at the heart of all Jesus' preaching. Jesus called the people of his day, and all of us as well, to the love of God, which completes our humanity as persons with God at the center of our lives, who love our neighbor as we love ourselves.

The proclamation of Jesus challenged the societal, ecclesiastical, and personal status quo of the people in his time. Jesus experienced rejection by his people, betrayal by his followers, and worst of all, a sense of abandonment by his God. Death on the cross was the price Jesus paid for his behavior and his message. The resurrection vindicates Jesus and verifies that God's faithfulness prevails.

This Jesus, with his message of God's nearness and the apparent impracticality of the life that message evokes, is shown to be the Son of God, and his message and ministry is confirmed as true and worthy of our trust. This is the Jesus to whom disciples are drawn and whom they are called to follow.

The Story of Jesus and the Hungers of Young People

Throughout history, the Church has been entrusted with proclaiming the story of Jesus, living the Good News, responding to the needs and hungers of the human family, and celebrating this relationship with Jesus in worship. In a multitude of ages, cultures, and settings, the reign of God continues to break through, affirming the diversity through which God speaks. Today, the reign of God is breaking through in the cultural experiences of young people, and the church is challenged to proclaim that breakthrough and to bring the Gospel of Jesus into dialogue with their story.

The world today, as in Jesus' day and on through history, sometimes seems dominated by the clear effects of a broken relationship with God: war, oppression, poverty, racism, sexism, materialism, and hopelessness. In recognizing such personal and social sin, we begin to realize that, indeed, today's world is as much in need of salvation as it was in Jesus' time. Within this context, young people yearn for a sense of hope and fulfillment in their individual lives.

Young people hunger for healing in their personal, individual lives, as well as in their relationships, families, and communities. A full understanding of the salvation offered by Jesus speaks to all of these dimensions. The Christian conviction is that Jesus and his message free us from sin, bind us in love, and call us to fullness in

God both as individuals and as a community. In the Church's ministry among young people today, our response to this call to love must be grounded in the acknowledgment of the hungers of today's adolescents.

The Hunger for Meaning and Purpose

One of the great fears of young people is that much of life simply does not matter, that life is not grounded in meaning. They fear that their families, their relationships, their church, their future, and even their lives do not matter. One challenge of youth ministry, therefore, is to provide a Gospel vision of life that identifies and calls into question the false messages contemporary society gives about what it means to be human. Meaning and purpose are found in the call to love, which is the fullness of our humanity, centered in God and expressed in the love of others.

The Hunger for Connection

Young people have a strong need for relationships, for connecting with others on a variety of levels. It is within these connections that love and acceptance are experienced. Ideally, the family is the primary and foundational experience of such connectedness. It is within a healthy family that a child first experiences love, security, and belonging. Young people, then, move toward further connection with their peer group and in individual relationships where acceptance and friendship are experienced. Eventually, young people come to see themselves as connected to the larger communities of school, church, and society. A major challenge we face, therefore, is to provide a faith community of acceptance, belonging, and welcome, where young people can hear the Good News proclaimed and see the Gospel lived out.

The Hunger for Recognition

Young people experience a fundamental need to feel worthwhile and important. This need is met when they experience the attention and interest of others, providing the basis for self-esteem and self-confidence. Young people need to be affirmed in their goodness and in their giftedness. They need to be appreciated and loved. They need to be listened to. Through relationships of trust, acceptance, and understanding, through experiences of feeling connected to others and to the community, through knowing that God indeed pays attention and cares for them, young people feel better about themselves, come to self-acceptance, and are enabled to reach out to others.

The Hunger for Justice

The hunger for justice is perhaps the least obvious of the hungers of young people but still very present in the lives of many of them. From the earliest days of childhood, we hear the cry of "That's not fair!" There is an innate sense and desire for justice and fairness in young people. They are quick to point out the inequities of life in the distribution of goods, possessions, and even opportunities. Directly and indirectly, they experience violence, hatred, and hurt. Our challenge is to not let this hunger for justice succumb to the societal pressures of materialism, consumerism, and individualism. The Gospel calls us to a vision where all have access to the goods and resources of the world, where the poor and the marginalized become a priority, and where justice and peace are signs that the reign of God has broken through.

The Hunger for the Holy

Research demonstrates clearly that many young people experience a spiritual vacuum. They often see a gap between professed belief and actual practice in the faith community, and they frequently experience a church whose teachings seem to be out of touch with their real, lived situations. However, young people continue to search for a faith that makes sense, that provides direction and meaning, and that challenges. They are looking for a language to help them understand their experiences of God, searching for ways to deepen their experiences of the sacred, and seeking a community of people with whom to journey. Young people are looking for a worthwhile adventure. Joining with Jesus in work on behalf of the reign of God he proclaimed is that adventure. Our challenge is to be a community of believers and disciples that invites, welcomes, loves, and involves young people in building up the reign of God.

Jesus never backed off from the challenge of responding to the hungers of the people of his day. Rather, he sought ways to transform the situations and lives of people. Jesus often referred to and built upon their concerns, experiences, and symbols in his teaching, healing, and serving. In the evangelization of young people, we are challenged to do the same. We must confront and transform those situations that bind our young people, and we must free them for the fullness of their humanity. We must begin with their experiences, their symbols, and their hungers, if our efforts in proclaiming the nearness of the reign of God are to be fruitful.

Principles of Catholic Youth Evangelization

We can identify certain principles that are rooted in the Foundations of Catholic Youth Evangelization and flow from our understanding of effective youth ministry. These foundational and operational principles provide a framework for our efforts in the evangelization of young people in various local communities. These principles are interrelated and are not given in any priority order in the lists that follow.

The foundational principles point to key understandings about the nature and context of youth evangelization. The operational principles describe guidelines for developing this multidimensional ministry. Commentary on each of these principles follows the respective list offered here.

Foundational Principles

The following principles are basic in understanding youth evangelization.

- The starting point for youth evangelization is our recognition of the presence of God already in young people, their experiences, their families, and their culture.
- In the evangelization of youth, we must consider the developmental characteristics of young people.
- Evangelization efforts must support families in their role as the primary evangelizers of their children.
- Evangelization is the responsibility of the entire faith community.
- Evangelization draws on and responds to the richness of individual ethnic cultures.
- Evangelization recognizes the power of society to shape the values and identities of young people.

Commentary

The starting point for youth evangelization is our recognition of the presence of God already in young people, their experiences, their families, and their culture.

Through the Incarnation of God in Jesus, Christians are convinced that divinity is present within and through all of creation, and, in a special way, within humanity. Evangelization, therefore, enables young people to uncover and name the experience of a God already active and present in their lives. This provides openness to the gift of the Good News of Jesus Christ. In this way the experiences of young people can be recognized as religiously significant. God is experienced in the ordinary happenings of our lives, in the relationships of family, and in the rituals and traditions of culture.

In the evangelization of youth, we must consider the developmental characteristics of young people.

Much research has been done on the developmental needs and characteristics of early, middle, and late adolescents. Our efforts in evangelization must take into account the appropriate life tasks of young people at their particular stage of personal and social development. The same is true for the faith development of young people.

A schema describing various styles of faith and the focus of our evangelizing efforts is useful here. One such schema, as described in *Will Our Children Have Faith?* (New York: Morehouse Group, 2000), by John H. Westerhoff III, suggests that faith is reflected in the life of Christians in four different styles.

The first style, *experienced faith,* is most commonly recognized as the faith of children. It is essentially a matter of their developing faith by coming into contact with and then imitating the faith convictions and activities of people around them, especially in the family. Evangelization responsive to this style of faith must center on welcoming families and individuals into the community.

The second style, *affiliative faith,* is characterized by a need for belonging and participating in the community. The community provides the shape and content of faith. Evangelization in this case must concentrate on welcoming and inviting youth into the community. Therefore, evangelization responsive to this style is a ministry of fostering community, hospitality, and welcome. Ministers assuming this role as representatives of the community might think of themselves as "adoption agents," trying to offer a sense of home to young people.

The third style, *searching faith,* signals the young person's more conscious movement towards a personal, freely embraced faith. This style is characterized by a time of questioning and of challenging previously held beliefs and testing the community's story. The searching style of faith requires evangelizing efforts that provide opportunities for young people to grapple with their faith questions within a supportive community. During this time the role of the minister is to be a "midwife," enabling young people to give birth to their personal faith identity while they dialogue with the community's story in Scripture and Tradition.

Owned faith, the fourth style, reflects the culmination or full fruition of this process of faith growth. Owned faith is characterized by one's witness to faith by word and action and is lived out through an integrated lifestyle. It is only within the context of owned faith that the call to full discipleship can be most clearly heard by Christians. Knowing that this style of faith is characteristic primarily in young adulthood or later, our evangelizing efforts must adjust accordingly. This is not to suggest, however, that younger adolescents should not be called to discipleship. Rather, at earlier ages, the call to discipleship is conditioned by the young person's personal and faith development and his or her situation in life. This call must be developmentally appropriate, and our expectations must be realistic and sensitive.

This process of maturing in faith is not a linear one. Westerhoff likens the process to a tree that grows and expands, its growth marked by rings that build on previous rings. Faith, as it grows and expands, builds on the previous styles of faith. But the needs and characteristics of the styles are never left behind. Rather, like the rings of a tree, they are always present, forming the foundation for the next developing style.

Evangelization efforts must support families in their role as the primary evangelizers of their children.

The Church of today is making a special effort to call the family to a very important and primary evangelizing role with their children. We address young people and their families within a variety of settings, structures, and contexts. Given the critical impact that parents' faith expression has on the faith of their children, our efforts must support parents as the primary evangelizers of their children.

Therefore, evangelizing the family as a unit is an important task. Because the family is an interconnected system, changes in any one member affect all the others. For example, in families where a young person is evangelized but the rest of the family is not, there exists the possibility of tension between them and even mutual rejection. On the other hand, the evangelization of the young person could well spark curiosity and interest in the faith on the part of all other family members. In either case, evangelization efforts must look to the welfare of the entire family.

The family as domestic church should be recognized as a partner with other dimensions of church in fostering faith among adolescents. There should be a mutuality in this partnership in which each supports the efforts of the other. The wider faith community supports the family by providing services such as parent enrichment and family programs and parenting skills education.

On the family's part, young people's faith is nurtured and enhanced through family celebrations and rituals, the faith-modeling and daily witness of the parents, and shared family prayer. The family and the broader faith community are both settings in which young people can be challenged to examine their values.

Evangelization is the responsibility of the entire faith community.

Young people today belong to a variety of communities, including the family as their primary community. During adolescence, their most influential faith community may be their parish, their Catholic school, some other youth-serving organization, or a combination of these. Still, the responsibility for the ministry remains with the entire community, while recognizing that certain persons may be designated to coordinate and implement the community's ministry to youth.

Critical to evangelization is the life of the faith community. The most effective evangelizing and outreach to young people is that which is supported and grounded in the vibrant life of the community, while integrating young people fully into the life and ministry of the community.

The community's liturgical celebrations, sacramental life, social ministry outreach, catechetical programs, and other ministry activities, as well as the community's posture of welcome and hospitality, are vitally important in making the faith community the living proclamation of the Good News. Evangelization is very effective when the participation of young people in all of these ministerial efforts is valued and they, therefore, feel important to the community.

In some situations, of course, the life of the faith community is less than vibrant, and the invitation to responsible participation is not effectively or genuinely extended. In such cases, the individual relationships formed between young people and particular caring, believing adults take on an increased importance. These relationships may develop into a small "base community" for young people and enable them to feel connected to the church.

Evangelization draws on and responds to the richness of individual ethnic cultures.

The Gospel of Jesus comes to every culture as the in-breaking of the reign of God, with its grace-filled offer of salvation and its promise of renewed life in Christ. Viewed theologically, the social phenomenon of enculturation finds its source and inspiration in the mystery of the Incarnation. Enculturation is the interpenetration of the reign of God and its expression in the Gospel message within the expressions and life of all cultures. It is the concrete embodiment that the Word assumes in a particular individual, community, or culture. Through authentic enculturation, Christ becomes concretely alive in that culture.

The evangelization of youth, therefore, takes place within the diversity of cultural experiences of the church in North America. Efforts in evangelization must honor and respect the various faith styles and traditions of the cultural communities in which young people live. These various expressions of the faith underscore the richness of the Gospel, even while the Gospel critiques the individual cultures.

With their common emphasis on family, community, ritual expression, and tradition, ethnic cultures contribute to our efforts in the evangelization of young people. We need to incorporate the symbols, stories, and rituals of traditional ethnic cultures and contemporary youth experiences into our efforts towards the proclamation of the Gospel.

Evangelization recognizes the power of society to shape the values and identities of young people.

Our efforts in evangelization take place within the context of mainstream society. Contemporary culture powerfully impacts young people, sending messages about the basic meanings of life, relationships, and one's self-definition. Though contemporary society can have a positive and Christian impact on young people, certain aspects of society must certainly be recognized as non-Christian. The Gospel is essentially counter-cultural. The Gospel values of harmony, service, and community stand in stark contrast to the violence, consumerism, and extreme individualism of contemporary U.S. culture.

Additionally, differences certainly exist between the rural, suburban, and urban experiences, adding to the complexity and impact of culture. It is, therefore, a "sign of the times" that the Gospel must stand in dialogue with all these aspects of society, critiquing and transforming them where necessary.

> For the Church, evangelizing means bringing the Good News into all strata of humanity, and through its influence transforming humanity from within and making it new. . . . [The Church] evangelizes when she seeks to convert, solely through the divine power of the Message she proclaims, both the personal and collective consciences of people, the activities in which they engage, and the lives and concrete milieus which are theirs. (*Evangelii Nuntiandi,* no. 18)

Operational Principles

Each of the operational principles has a personal or individual element. At times, evangelization is the activity of one individual directed towards another. Young people must be called through the invitation of other believers, personally and individually, into a relationship with Jesus.

At the same time, the operational principles have a communal dimension. The Church as the community of believers, through its outreach, pastoral services, and sacramental life, does evangelize individuals, proclaiming the Gospel message and inviting the hearer into the community. Additionally, the Church calls for the transformation of the broader cultural and societal communities, as described in the foundational principles.

Both the personal and the communal aspects must be considered in implementing effective approaches to youth evangelization.

We identify the following operational principles, which are further described below:

- Evangelization has an explicit dimension.
- Evangelization has an implicit dimension.
- Evangelization involves an initial proclamation.
- Evangelization involves an ongoing proclamation.
- Evangelization requires that the Church be physically present in the real situations of young people's lives.
- Evangelization recognizes moments of hurt, need, and crisis as significant entry points for proclaiming the Good News of Jesus and for making real the healing power of God.
- Evangelization calls young people to live daily as disciples of Jesus.
- Evangelization must be integrated into the comprehensive youth ministry efforts of the faith community.

Commentary

Evangelization has an explicit dimension.

Our ministry to young people needs to include the explicit verbal proclamation of the Good News. Youth need to literally *hear* the Good News of Jesus. "There is no true evangelization if the name, the teaching, the life, the promises, the kingdom and the mystery of Jesus of Nazareth, the Son of God, are not proclaimed" (*Evangelii Nuntiandi,* no. 22).

Through vibrant liturgical celebrations, parish youth missions, retreats and reflection days, public proclamation, adolescent catechesis programs, youth rallies and conferences, and other means, young people need to hear about Jesus and his message. The community needs to "tell the story" of Jesus.

Evangelization has an implicit dimension.

Perhaps the first step in evangelization is "earning the right to be heard." In youth ministry, this important step is commonly identified as outreach or relationship building. The development of relationships of acceptance, trust, and respect is critical if young people are to ever truly "hear" the Good News. Without such a relational foundation, our efforts to proclaim the message of Jesus will be experienced by young people as "a noisy gong or a clanging cymbal" (1 Cor. 13:1).

Evangelization, therefore, has a nonverbal dimension in that ministers to young people are called first to be visible signs of God's love. We are challenged to "be the story" in the flesh for young people. As the time-tested phrase puts it, "We may be the only Gospel some young people ever read." Our relationships with youth should reflect our personal understanding and love of Jesus, our own growth in faith, and mirror the kind of relationships Jesus established with those with whom he had contact.

Further, this implicit dimension is expressed through the minister's lifestyle. "Above all, the Gospel must be proclaimed by witness. . . . Such a witness is already a silent proclamation of the Good News and a very powerful and effective one" (*Evangelii Nuntiandi,* no. 21). We are challenged to live the Good News in every aspect of our daily life: family, work, worship, service, and play. In so doing, the Good News will be proclaimed through all we are and in all we do.

There is also a communal dimension to this principle. The credibility of the minister to youth hinges on the acceptance and support of him or her by the community. The life of the community must give witness to the transforming power of the Good News. The faith community, too, is challenged to "be the story." The qualities of the evangelizing community are further described in ["The Evangelizing Community," later in this document].

Evangelization involves an initial proclamation.

Within the entire faith journey, evangelization is the starting point, whether in its explicit or implicit dimension. It is the initial proclamation of the Good News of the reign of God that calls young people into a relationship with Jesus Christ, calls for a change of heart, and invites them into the community of believers.

This initial proclamation is implicit when centered in the relationships that develop between adult Christians and young people. The initial proclamation is explicit when young people literally "hear" for the first time the Good News of Jesus Christ. For many young people this occurs in the family prior to any contact with formal or systematic youth ministry efforts. However, for other young people who "have eyes to see and ears to hear," our efforts in evangelization, whether implicit or explicit, can become the starting point for a continuing, lifelong faith journey.

Evangelization involves an ongoing proclamation.

For many young people, the Church's efforts in evangelization are ongoing in that they support the faith already initiated in the family. Throughout the faith journey the proclamation of the Good News needs to be repeated and resounded. All our ministerial efforts need to be infused with the proclamation of the Good News. The Good News is news that needs to be heard and seen—explicitly through word and implicitly through witness—over and over again.

The need for ongoing evangelization is especially intense for young people, given their ongoing personal, relational, and faith development. Throughout their development they need to hear anew of Jesus and the Gospel message. For many, regardless of their participation and involvement in the faith community, it is impossible to determine when the Good News is first really "heard" or when it first impacts their heart. But whenever that initial "hearing" takes place, the Good News, for many young people, needs to be repeatedly proclaimed as new, given the changes and challenges in their personal, familial, faith, and relational worlds.

Evangelization requires that the church be physically present in the real situations of young people's lives.

Whether implicit or explicit, the proclamation of the Good News includes a question of geography. Effective evangelization demands that the church be where young people are. We need to be in their settings: their neighborhoods, their homes, their schools, their workplaces, the malls, the street corners, wherever young people gather—at appropriate times and in appropriate ways. This is a most effective way to build relationships that support, challenge, heal, and guide. When the Church is willing to be where young people are, we communicate to youth that they are important. That message, too, is a proclamation of good news.

Evangelization recognizes moments of hurt, need, and crisis as significant entry points for proclaiming the Good News of Jesus and making real the healing power of God.

Those who minister among young people must listen carefully to their often painful stories. In so doing, we become avenues for Jesus' compassion, healing, hope, and reconciliation for young people who may be hurting and alienated.

In addition to the normal settings in which we minister, and building on the previous operational principle, being avenues of compassion requires that the Church, through our efforts, also be present to young people in those social service situations where they frequently deal with their difficult personal, familial, and social issues. There are times and situations when we need to physically be the Good News, implicitly and explicitly, for young people who cannot come to us and our settings.

Evangelization calls young people to live daily as disciples of Jesus.

Young people must be challenged to undertake the mission of love, prayer, witness, outreach, and Gospel proclamation themselves. Our efforts in evangelizing must contain an invitation to "responsible participation in the life, mission and work of the faith community" (*A Vision of Youth Ministry,* p. 7).

However, this call to discipleship—to taking on the values, actions, and qualities of Jesus—is conditioned by young people's personal and faith development and their situation in life. The principle of "developmental discipleship" requires that the call to mission and the response of young people be age appropriate and that our expectations be realistic.

Evangelization must be integrated into the comprehensive youth ministry efforts of the faith community.

The invitation to relationship with Jesus and the community of believers is best extended and most readily accepted when situated within a holistic approach to young people. Through the youth ministry components of word, worship, community building, justice and service, guidance and healing, enablement, and advocacy, we foster a ministry that is to, with, by, and for young people. Comprehensive youth ministry enhances the development of a faith community in which the proclamation of the Good News is especially powerful.

Evangelization, therefore, must be an integral aspect of all components of comprehensive youth ministry. The integration of evangelization into all our youth ministry efforts will include its explicit and implicit dimensions, the initial and ongoing proclamation of the Good News, as well as the call to discipleship. This integration is described in fuller detail later in this document.

The operational principles clearly point out the "both/and" nature of evangelization. Effective evangelization certainly is a ministry in its own right. At the same time, evangelization needs to be infused into the entire effort of youth ministry in a faith community.

Evangelization must also be seen through both the personal and the communal lenses, as well as be implemented with a family and cultural perspective. Evangelization of young people is, indeed, a rich ministry, with varied starting points, dimensions, and approaches.

Dynamics of Catholic Youth Evangelization

Efforts in Catholic evangelization of young people include the elements of witness, outreach, proclamation, invitation, conversion, and the call to discipleship. Theoretically, these elements can be seen as taking place sequentially. However, evangelization is rarely a linear process. The following discussion should be viewed in that light.

Witness

Christian witness is the expression of our commitment to Christ and his Gospel and of our conviction in the promise of the reign of God. It is the daily living out of our baptismal commitment and membership in the faith community, and it is reflected in all areas of our life: family, neighborhood, workplace, school, and where we play and pray.

> To evangelize is first of all to bear witness, in a simple and direct way, to God revealed by Jesus Christ in the Holy Spirit, to bear witness that in His Son, God has loved the world—that in His Incarnate Word He has given being to all things and called men to eternal life. (*Evangelii Nuntiandi,* no. 26)

This witness contributes to and draws upon the vision and spiritual health of the local faith community. Further, this witness is observed by young people, often unbeknownst to the faith community. Young people do indeed watch us, checking to see if our faith truly "works" for us and if faith helps us to find meaning in our own lives. Therefore, the life and practice of the community give witness to the presence of the Spirit active in all its members.

Outreach

Intentional outreach, in a ministry sense, goes beyond daily witness. Outreach occurs when a believer becomes personally present to young people on their physical and psychological turf in order to respond to their real needs. Outreach requires that the faith community, through its ministers, be present in appropriate ways to young people in their situations (e.g., in their households, on school grounds, in their workplaces, on the streets, in their neighborhoods, in other social service institutions that minister to youth, and so on). Outreach signals a willingness by church ministers to spend time with young people, to listen to their stories, and to respond to their needs and concerns.

Outreach is a ministry to unbaptized youth as well as to baptized young people who are "unchurched" or not actively engaged in the life of the faith community. This is an important dimension in efforts to invite the unbaptized young people into the faith community. However, we also need to reach out to those baptized young people who are already present in our faith community but are "un-Gospeled"—those who have not really heard the Good News or experienced the joy, peace, and love of the Gospel. These young people, too, need to experience the power of the Good News and need to be brought forth in their faith.

Integral to outreach is its relational nature. In Christian outreach, believers place their faith story and their time at the service of young people's pain, loneliness, and questions. Our relationships with young people are visible signs that God cares for them. Outreach mirrors Jesus' contact with the marginalized, the poor, and the lonely. Effective Christian outreach has the following characteristics:

- Outreach is a visible, human sign of God's love for young people.
- Outreach requires that we be physically present on youths' turf.
- Outreach is a genuine response to needs that includes an invitation to participate in the faith of a caring community of believers; it is not merely a recruitment strategy or membership drive.

- Outreach is intended for young people who are unchurched or outside the faith community and also for those young people in the community who are in need of the healing care and concern of others.

Outreach is a critical and foundational element in the evangelization process. Therefore, the community must become more intentional in reaching beyond our familiar boundaries in order to reach those young people outside the normal ministerial settings.

Proclamation

While daily witness and intentional outreach are essential forms of implicit evangelization, Catholic evangelization remains incomplete if the Gospel is not explicitly proclaimed, both initially and on an ongoing basis. Without explicit proclamation of the essentials of the Good News, there "is no true evangelization" (*Evangelii Nuntiandi,* no. 22).

Whether implicitly or explicitly, the Good News must be proclaimed to young people. We are challenged and privileged to proclaim the Good News of Jesus and it is news that brings joy to the hearer! "I have said these things to you so that my joy may be in you, and that your joy may be complete" (John 15:11).

The message of the Christ Event is, indeed, good news: the news of God's powerful, saving love and Jesus as the ultimate revelation of that love. Jesus Christ is the Good News; he is the embodiment of God's all-embracing love.

At Easter, after the resurrection, the Church's proclamation of hope was first made, and it can enthusiastically be made again today. The Creator is not faceless and remote. God has been seen and known in human experience as Jesus, one crucified and raised to new life. Jesus has significance in all times and cultures, the Creator's definitive Word revealed.

The Good News came to its climax in the death and resurrection of Jesus. His death was the supreme expression of God's love for humanity. Jesus' resurrection is the vindication of his message and the guarantee of God's intention to raise everyone from the death of sin, from enslavement to anything that alienates us from God's saving love, and from death itself.

This is the incomparable Good News: God loves us and wants us to be happy. All we have to do is "believe in the good news" (Mark 1:15), that is, accept trustingly the Good News of God's saving love and then live lives that express our gratitude and joy.

There are several key themes in this Good News that are especially pertinent to young people today:

A God who loves us. The doctrine of the Incarnation tells us that "the Word became flesh and lived among us" (John 1:14). Jesus Christ is God and is, therefore, the most complete revelation of God. Jesus' life and ministry reveal a compassionate God. Young people need to hear of this God who cares and loves individually and specifically. Mistaken or false images of God must be replaced with one of a God who is actively present and involved in the lives of our young people.

Healing our humanity. Jesus offers healing and forgiveness of sin to those whom he encounters. That offer needs to be communicated to our young people. Jesus can heal the gaps that are so prevalent in the lives of many young people. He can heal the breakdowns in youths' personal relationships, in their families, in themselves, and in their relationship with God. Jesus and his message can bring forgiveness and healing to youths' pains and wounds, revealing the power of God's love.

The message and ministry of Jesus. To embrace God's love as proclaimed and lived by Jesus is to accept the values that Jesus taught. "I give you a new commandment, that you love one another. Just as I have loved you, you also should love one another. By this everyone will know that you are my disciples, if you have love for one another" (John 13:34–35). The love to which Jesus calls young people is not a vague feeling but a very practical and visible concern and care for all and especially those who are neglected or oppressed by others. This compassion is integral to being a disciple of Jesus. We are challenged to enable young people to understand the meaning of discipleship and to invite them to respond as youthful and energetic disciples of Jesus Christ.

A community of believers. The journey of faith has both a personal and a communal dimension. Young people certainly need to search through their faith questions, but they are invited to do so with the support of the faith community. Young people are invited to join a community that strives to witness to authentic discipleship through its community life, personal prayer and community celebration, lifelong growth in faith, and lives of justice, service, and peace. This is a community that celebrates its beliefs in and through its sacramental life, a celebration that culminates in the Eucharist.

> In the dynamism of evangelization, a person who accepts the Church as the Word which saves, normally translates it into the following sacramental acts: adherence to the Church and acceptance of the Sacraments, which manifest and support this adherence through the grace they confer. (*Evangelii Nuntiandi,* no. 23)

These themes only touch upon the wealth and depth of Catholic belief. Whichever themes we choose to integrate into our local ministry with young people, it is essential that young people come to see the Gospel as speaking to their lived experiences in their very real settings.

This challenge to "tell the story" refers not only to the initial proclamation of the Good News but also to a proclamation that is continually coming forth from the entire life of the faith community.

Invitation

As elements of the process of evangelization, effective witness and outreach should, in effect, extend an invitation to youth to a personal relationship with Jesus and with the community that follows him. The sense of acceptance and trust sparked by effective witness and outreach makes credible the invitation to full participation in the community of believers, where the proclamation of the Good News can take on its full power.

When the community exhibits a genuine sense of welcome and hospitality, the invitation to belonging is implicitly extended. However, there is a need, especially with young people, to explicitly invite their participation in the community. This invitation is most effective when it is individual and specific and offered in the context of caring and accepting relationships. We need to be intentional in personally inviting young people into the life and mission of the faith community. Additionally, we must develop strategies that enable the community to mirror Jesus' invitation to "come and see."

Conversion

Evangelization rightly finds its full development when witness, outreach, proclamation, and invitation enable young people to "change their heart" and to participate more fully in the life and mission of the church community. Conversion refers to this change in heart. In Scripture and theology, this change is referred to as a *metanoia*. In the context of this document, conversion is the ongoing, lifelong process of turning away from conditions, actions, and attitudes that lessen human and spiritual growth, and turning more and more towards Jesus and his values and teachings.

Conversion is a critical dimension in the process of evangelization. The process of conversion includes one's fundamental decision to be open to the presence of the Holy Spirit and to admit God into one's life. In youth ministry circles, this pivotal decision is often referred to as "the aha moment" or "the moment of recognition." Such a "peak experience" in the lifelong process of conversion is often the beginning of free and active solidarity with the purposes of the reign of God in the world. We must, in appropriate ways, call young people to make a decision about Jesus and about participation in the building of the reign of God.

For the unbaptized, this call may lead to sacramental initiation into the community. For the already baptized, the ongoing process of conversion leads to a maturing of faith through the full and faithful reception of the sacraments, engagement in catechesis, and acceptance of the Christian mandate to serve the Church and all humanity (cf. *Evangelii Nuntiandi,* nos. 23–24). Fostering the process of conversion, therefore, requires increased collaboration in local faith communities between youth ministry and RCIA programs.

Evangelization, therefore, includes an explicit invitation to young people to engage in a growing relationship with Jesus through ongoing conversion and participation in the community of believers, and it challenges them to a lifestyle that is in accord with the Gospel.

The Call to Discipleship

Full membership in the church requires that one undertake the mission of the community. This is the call to be a disciple of Jesus.

The word *disciple* meaning "learner" or "student," describes both the individual's and the community's relationship with Jesus. There are several distinct elements in this understanding of discipleship:

Discipleship involves a personal call and a personal response. In the Gospels, Jesus says, "Come, follow me." This call, when it is totally unexpected, causing disruption and confusion in our lives, is perhaps best reflected in the story of Paul. At other times, the call is more gradual, a process of awakening to the meaning of the Gospel in our lives. However it is experienced, Jesus' call requires a personal and ongoing response.

Discipleship requires a holistic response. The notion of following Jesus entails more than one aspect of our lives; being a disciple touches everything about us—our values, our choices, the use of our resources, and our dreams. "Discipleship involves imitating the pattern of Jesus' life by openness to God's will in the service of others" (USCCB, "Economic Justice for All," no. 47). The heart of discipleship is this call to shape our lives in the vision, values, and teachings of Jesus.

Discipleship requires the change of heart and change of perspective described in the Scriptures as a "metanoia." A metanoia is a change in our entire view of reality, looking at God and all of life through the values and vision of Jesus expressed in the Gospel. This moment in the conversion process is the first step into the life of the Trinity and into active participation in the kingdom, the reign of God that Jesus proclaims.

Discipleship has a distinctly communal dimension. Christian discipleship includes an invitation to life within a community of believers. "To be a Christian is to join with others in responding to this personal call and in learning the meaning of Christ's life" ("Economic Justice for All," no. 46). For young people this community of believers includes their family, their friends, the parish, the diocese, other local faith communities, and the universal church.

Mission is the final element integral to discipleship. To be a disciple of Jesus is to take up his mission—the mission of establishing the reign of God. Young people are called to participate in Jesus' mission, now the mission of the faith community. Through witness, outreach, service to others, and living the Good News in all aspects of their lives—in their family, school, neighborhood, and community—young people live out their discipleship and participate in the mission of Jesus.

Accepting and responding to the call to discipleship is the culmination of the process of evangelization. However, the dynamics of evangelization are interrelated, and the process itself is cyclic in nature. Witnessing to the Good News is always an important aspect of daily Christian living. Intentional outreach to unchurched or un-Gospeled young people is an ongoing challenge. The proclamation of the Good News is continual, and the invitation into relationship is constantly renewed. Conversion, too, is a cyclic process that takes place again and again as turning points and "aha moments" recur in the lifelong process of growth in relationship with Jesus and the community of believers. All these elements together result in a lifestyle of discipleship.

Integration of Evangelization and Catholic Youth Ministry

Evangelization cannot be packaged into a neat program. It is first and foremost an attitude, a commitment, even a fervor, that becomes the energizing core of our ministry efforts with young people. The proclamation of the Good News is most effective when integrated into a comprehensive approach to youth ministry. *A Vision of Youth Ministry* provides a framework for developing this approach to ministry with young people.

The components of a holistic youth ministry, as described in the *Vision* document, are interdependent. When viewed through a single lens, they provide a complete picture of Catholic youth ministry's field of action. Naturally, the youth ministry agenda and goals will vary from place to place, depending on the needs and resources in each unique local situation. However, there are many creative ways in which local parishes, schools, and other faith communities evangelize young people through the components of youth ministry.

Ministry of the Word

Catechesis is a vital expression of the ministry of the word. Evangelization and catechesis are closely related. In fact, a desire to evangelize is at the heart of adolescent catechesis. Effective programs of adolescent catechesis are vital in strengthening and deepening young people's response to the proclamation of the Good News. These opportunities build upon the initial phases of evangelization—Christian witness, outreach, proclamation, and conversion—by explaining Gospel truths fully and enthusiastically. Therefore, catechesis flows from and enhances foundational evangelizing activities.

Systematic catechesis presents opportunities for evangelization through the faith witness of catechists, Scripture sharing, storytelling, confirmation preparation programs, and breaking open the values and teachings of Jesus. The challenge for those in the catechetical programs of youth ministry is to enable young people to apply the Good News to their lived situations and to help them examine the implications of discipleship. To be effective in meeting this challenge, catechetical programs will utilize culturally appropriate resources and encourage the sharing of faith among young people.

Ministry of Worship

In the wider faith community, young people experience the faith and prayerfulness of a celebrating church. Meaningful youth liturgies and intergenerational worship experiences include the proclamation of the Good News and the celebration of the sacraments.

These experiences challenge young people to grow in faith, as well as serve to nurture that growth.

A church that is a spiritual homeland provides worship that is inclusive of all, authentically Catholic, and utilizes the gifts of diverse ethnic cultures. Liturgies of the word, the sacrament of reconciliation, and the Eucharist need to be celebrated regularly. Homilies that are full of life and relevance to young people's experiences are indispensable for effective evangelization. Youth need to experience the full ritual expressions of our sacraments and to be active participants in the celebration of those sacraments.

Our youth ministry events should include opportunities for various types of individual and communal prayer. The ministry of worship presents opportunities for evangelization through vibrant liturgy, bold proclamation of the Good News, and personal and communal prayer experiences. Those in youth ministry are also challenged to involve young people in worship experiences, utilize the young peoples' symbols and music, and teach young people various ways to pray.

Ministry of Community Building

Through witness, outreach, hospitality, and a genuine sense of welcome, young people are invited into the Christian community, in which their faith can be nurtured. A community of believers best enables young people to experience deeply the Good News by nurturing a sense of belonging and acceptance, a sense of "being home" in the parish, in the diocese, and in the universal Church.

This ministry of community building requires opportunities for evangelization through person-to-person contacts, social gatherings, peer relationships, group-building strategies, and celebrations in a Gospel-centered spirit of hospitality. Further, intergenerational and family-centered experiences contribute to this sense of community.

Those involved in youth ministry are challenged to make our communities more welcoming and inclusive for young people, for the poor, for strangers, and for various ethnic and cultural groups. We are challenged to develop communities that exhibit, express, and live the Gospel message and the call to discipleship.

Ministry of Justice and Service

The Gospel compels each of us to reach out in the name of Jesus Christ and to be a living sign of hope in the reign of God. As young people hear the call to discipleship, they should be encouraged to put their gifts, skills, and talents at the service of God's human family and all the world.

This ministry of justice and service is an opportunity for evangelization when our approaches are infused with Scripture and Jesus' teachings. Immersion experiences, service projects, and justice education programs present opportunities for youth to see the face of Jesus in the marginalized, oppressed, and poor. The challenge for those in youth ministry is to enable young people to bring the Gospel into a transforming dialogue with society and culture.

Ministry of Guidance and Healing

The ministry of guidance and healing involves personal, spiritual, and vocational guidance. We provide opportunities for young people's holistic growth, peer ministry, family outreach, and information on critical issues facing young people. Experiences of woundedness provide a natural entry point for the healing power of God. Often, in the midst of these experiences, young people are most open to the liberating and freeing message of the Gospel.

The component of guidance and healing presents opportunities for evangelization through individual relationships of caring, listening and support, sharing the healing message of Jesus, and sacramental reconciliation. We are challenged to reach out to young people in crisis, to confront their "at-risk" issues and behaviors, and to bring the message and power of the Gospel to their real situations.

Ministry of Enablement

Those in youth ministry are called to foster the gifts, talents, and skills of young people and provide opportunities for their use for the good of the faith community and the larger society. Enablement presents opportunities for evangelization when young people themselves become evangelizers. Adolescents themselves are called to share the Good News in witness and in word. For young people, there is no more powerful witness than other young people's own stories of the presence and activity of God in their lives.

Scripture study, faith sharing, creating prayer experiences, peer witness training, retreat team training and other leadership formation approaches, participation as liturgical ministers, and evangelization skills formation all have an evangelization dimension. Those in youth ministry are challenged to create these opportunities, which enable young people to live and share their faith.

Ministry of Advocacy

We are called to advocate for young people and their needs and their gifts on all levels—family, school, culture, church, and the larger community. Those in youth ministry must take the initiative in raising the faith community's consciousness of their responsibility to young people. The faith community must be made fully aware of its duty to be inviting and welcoming to young people. The faith community should also be challenged to enable the meaningful participation of adolescents and their families in the mission and ministry of the church. The secular community must be challenged to respond adequately to youths' needs and to enable young people to use their gifts and talents for the good of others.

This component presents opportunities for evangelization when we remind the faith community of its mission and responsibility to welcome and involve young people as full members of the community. The faith community must provide resources, facilities, and staff for comprehensive youth ministry and implement this ministry in culturally appropriate ways. Those in ministry to youth are challenged to be faithful and credible witnesses to the presence of God in the lives of young people and to speak on behalf of youth whenever necessary.

We who share the responsibility for ministry to young people in the varied settings of the Church must continue to develop approaches and strategies for further integrating evangelization into the components of comprehensive youth ministry.

The Evangelizing Community

We have described how evangelization is the responsibility of the entire faith community.

> Who then has the mission of evangelizing? . . . By divine mandate, the duty of going out into the whole world and preaching the Gospel to every creature . . . is a basic duty of the People of God. (*Evangelii Nuntiandi,* no. 59)

Further, in communion with the universal Church,

> the individual Churches . . . have the task of assimilating the essence of the Gospel message and transposing it, without the slightest betrayal of its essential truth, into the language that these particular people understand, and then proclaiming it in this language. (*Evangelii Nuntiandi,* no. 63)

Effective evangelization of young people, therefore, requires that an evangelizing community proclaim the Good News in a language young people understand. In order to do so, the evangelizing community must possess certain characteristics.

Characteristics of the Evangelizing Community

There are particular characteristics that must be present in the faith community if the evangelization of young people is to be effective. The community must be one that does the following:

Celebrates the Story
The faith community, through vibrant liturgy, preaching, and prayer experiences, must celebrate the Jesus story and announce the reign of God.

Tells the Story
Through effective catechetical programs at all age levels, both systematic and informal, the faith community must be able to proclaim and explain the Good News and the traditions and beliefs of the church as the community of believers.

Is the Story

The faith community must give witness to the Good News through the authentic living of the Gospel. The community itself must exhibit the sense of joy, celebration, and acceptance characteristic of the early Christian communities. Additionally, the faith community must also be the story for the larger culture and society through its social ministry and outreach.

Welcomes and Offers Hospitality

The faith community must offer a genuine invitation to all young people and foster a sense of welcome and gracious hospitality.

Values Young People

The Church must be a faith community that expresses overt affection for youth. The Church must be a community that stands with young people; really listens to their dreams, hopes and insights; responds to their needs; calls forth their gifts; and celebrates with them.

Invites Responsible Participation

Young people must have a meaningful role in the life and ministry of the faith community. However, young people also need to be called to discipleship and to minister to the larger society and culture on behalf of the faith community.

Calls for the Involvement of Adults

The faith community must call forth caring, committed adults who want to minister to, with, and for young people. Integral to this ministry are adults who like young people, who are spiritually healthy and rooted in prayer, who live their faith, and who are open to ongoing, personal conversion. Adults who are able to share their faith story and who are willing to enter into relationships of mutual trust, acceptance, and respect are vital if the community is to minister effectively to young people.

Is Inclusive

The faith community must be inclusive on the basis of age, sex, economic status, family makeup, culture, and race in its membership, ministry, celebrations, and outreach. We must identify and call forth the gifts of the diverse cultures, races, and age groups present in our communities.

Provides Opportunities
and a Place for Youth to Gather

There is a need to provide opportunities for young people to gather together as a peer community in a welcoming and comfortable physical setting. Within this environment young people are able to share faith, satisfy personal and relational needs, and develop friendships.

Collaborative Partnerships

Evangelization will never be possible without the action of the Holy Spirit. The Spirit is the source of power and life behind all of the other agents. It must be said that the Holy Spirit is the principal agent of evangelization, for it is the Spirit who impels each individual to proclaim the Gospel, and it is the Spirit who in the depths of hearts causes the word of salvation to be accepted and understood. Through the Holy Spirit the Gospel penetrates to the heart of the world, for it is the Spirit "who causes people to discern the signs of the times," which evangelization reveals and puts to use within history (*Evangelii Nuntiandi,* no. 75). It is the Spirit who energizes the community for the task of evangelization.

Within the larger faith community there are various agents for evangelization that have impact on young people. These agents must be brought together in a holistic ministry to young people, requiring collaborative partnerships on behalf of evangelizing youth.

The Family

The family is the heart of both the human community and the faith community.

> The family has well deserved the beautiful name of "domestic Church." The family, like the Church, ought to be a place where the Gospel is transmitted and from which the Gospel radiates. In a family which is conscious of this mission, all the members evangelize and are evangelized. (*Evangelii Nuntiandi,* no. 71)

It is in the family where we first come to hear and know the name and mission of Jesus Christ. The family shares in the life and mission of the Church by becoming a believing and loving community. Those who witness the love and reconciling nature of

Christian families, as well as the spiritual life and the presence of Christ within those families, become the recipients of family evangelization. The family, therefore, reflects the living image of Jesus and transmits the values and traditions of a disciple of Christ.

The Parish

Incorporating the characteristics of the evangelizing community, the parish community dedicates itself under the Gospel to worship and to witness, to teach and to learn, to serve and to liberate, to welcome others and to extend itself for the sake of the reign of God.

Parishes should show forth the joy and hope that come to those who are disciples of Christ. This witness of faith by the parish community is an important evangelizing action. Therefore, all aspects of parish life have potential for evangelizing both those young people who are seeking a deeper spiritual life within the community and those who have not yet accepted or heard the call of Christ.

The Catholic School

The Catholic school, which has brought several generations of Catholics into a deeper understanding of the Good News of Jesus Christ, also serves as an agent for the evangelization of many young people. The Catholic school is often experienced as the primary faith community for those young people attending. Evangelization takes root when Catholic schools promote the dignity of each student; proclaim the Good News of Jesus; combat the roots of poverty, racism, and oppression; and prepare young people to bring the principles of truth and justice to the society in which they will live as adults. Catholic schools are challenged to integrate evangelization into their comprehensive campus ministry programs and into the life of the school. The faculty, staff, and students share in this responsibility.

Young People

Youth, too, are called to be evangelizers. "Young people who are well trained in faith and prayer must become more and more the apostles of youth. The Church counts greatly on their contribution" (*Evangelii Nuntiandi,* no. 72). Through their witness to the importance of faith in their lives, their expression of faith through service to others, and their participation in personal and communal prayer and worship, young people evangelize their peers. This is a most powerful agent for evangelization.

Leaders in Ministry

All Christian leaders share a responsibility for the evangelization of young people. However, those in direct ministry to youth have a special responsibility to create effective programs, activities, approaches, and outreach strategies that foster evangelization.

In whatever ministry setting we work—parish, school, diocesan office, community program, retreat program, social service agency, and so on—we have to commit to a collaborative approach. We need to initiate collaborative partnerships with the various faith communities that minister to young people. It is our task to provide the vision and direction for this ministry of evangelization.

An Invitation to Dialogue

The Holy Spirit must not only penetrate our present efforts in evangelization but also move us towards an honest examination of our current approach to the evangelization of young people. This examination is the first task for those responsible for the faith community's ministry to young people in all settings: parish, school, community, diocese, and other youth-serving organizations and programs. The following challenges must guide our efforts:

- We need to assess our current approaches to reaching out to unchurched and un-Gospeled young people.
- We need to shape a more inclusive, welcoming, and hospitable faith community.
- We need to improve the quality of worship experiences and involve young people more fully in their celebration.
- We need to integrate families into all of our evangelizing efforts.
- We need to examine our approaches to the explicit and implicit proclamation of the Good News.
- We need to support young people on their journey of faith and lifelong engagement in the process of conversion.
- We need to provide opportunities for high-quality, intentional catechesis, which fosters young people's knowledge and understanding of their faith and the church's traditions and teachings.

- We need to provide opportunities for our young people to respond to the call of discipleship.
- We need to integrate an evangelizing dimension in all components of our faith community's ministry to young people.

> (cf. *Go and Make Disciples: A National Plan and Strategy for Catholic Evangelization,* by the USCCB, nos. 89–127 at *www.usccb.org/evangelization/goandmake/eng.htm,* accessed October 13, 2004)

Diocesan offices of youth ministry, or those offices charged with ministry to young people, have a particular responsibility to provide training opportunities and resources for enhancing evangelization efforts in local youth ministry settings.

Diocesan offices also have opportunities to provide gathering events for young people that are occasions for evangelization. Diocesan youth conferences and rallies, diocesan service projects and work camps, youth missions or retreats, regional and national conferences, and the International Youth Days can all be very effective opportunities for young people to gather as church, to hear the word of God proclaimed and celebrated as a community of disciples.

All those in ministry with young people need to draw upon their expertise and their experiences and develop practical applications, models, strategies, approaches, and resources for the effective evangelization of young people. The entire faith community is now challenged to enter into dialogue on the issue of Catholic youth evangelization, so we can say, with St. Paul:

> "Everyone who calls on the name of the lord will be saved."
>
> But how are they to call on one in whom they have not believed? And how are they to believe in one of whom they have never heard? And how are they to hear without someone to proclaim him? And how are they to proclaim him unless they are sent? As it is written, "How beautiful are the feet of those who bring good news!" (Rom. 10:13–15)

Recommended Resources:
An Annotated Bibliography

Adolescent Catechesis: Resources from "The Living Light." United States Conference of Catholic Bishops, 2003. This compendium of articles focuses on the current issue of adolescent catechesis. Topics include evangelization, Confirmation, and athletics, by authors such as Mike Carotta, Maura and Mike Hagarty, and Mark Markuly.

The Bishops Respond: Prevention, Healing, and Resolve. United States Conference of Catholic Bishops, 2002. This pamphlet provides an overview of the key points covered in *The Charter for the Protection of Children and Young People.* In their pledge to safeguard the health and well-being of children, the bishops outline the new services and administrative structures required of all dioceses and the oversight that will ensure compliance with the new regulations.

Creating Safe and Sacred Places: Identifying, Preventing, and Healing Sexual Abuse. Gerard McGlone, Mary Shrader, and Laurie Delgatto. Saint Mary's Press, 2003. Ministry with young people begins by building relationships that include appropriate boundaries. *Creating Safe and Sacred Places* is the first resource of its kind in response to *The Charter for the Protection of Children and Youth* (issued by the United States Conference of Catholic Bishops). The charter calls, in part, for dioceses, schools, and parishes to establish "safe environment" programs. The manual provides information on procedures and strategies to promote a safe environment, including material for training parents, ministers, educators, and church personnel in identifying, preventing, and healing sexual abuse.

Effective Practices for Dynamic Youth Ministry. Thomas East, Ann Marie Eckert, Dennis Kurtz, and Brian Singer-Towns. Saint Mary's Press, 2004. This book, the result of research collaboration, outlines the proven strategies that have worked for the most successful Catholic youth ministry programs across the United States. Each chapter includes research results on best practices for youth ministry, quotes from youth and adults, and practical ideas for implementing successful youth programs.

General Directory for Catechesis. United States Conference of Catholic Bishops, 1998. The *GDC* includes a general definition of catechesis and its goals and essential elements, along with guidelines for drafting national catechisms and catechetical directories. For use in conjunction with the *Catechism of the Catholic Church*.

The Godbearing Life—The Art of Soul Tending in Youth Ministry. **Kenda Creasy Dean and Ron Foster. Upper Room Books, 1998.** The authors focus upon the necessity of having spiritual, youth relationships rather than just social, youth recreation. The crying need today is for churches to minister as only they can do to the emptiness young people face in their lives. Rather than competing with secular programming, Christian youth ministries are called to offer something entirely different from the secular world. The authors describe in detail various measures that will energize youth in their Christian faith. This title is far from a book of programming ideas but is rather a very readable volume of philosophy and theology on youth ministry.

Growing Teen Disciples: Strategies for Really Effective Youth Ministry. **Frank Mercadante. Saint Mary's Press, 2002.** Based on a solid spiritual foundation of prayer and the call to discipleship, the book explores ways to develop dynamic adult leaders, evangelize youth, provide spiritual formation, and develop teen leadership. Youth ministers of all skill levels will find inspiration and practical tools within the pages of this book.

Hiring for Youth Ministry: A Process for Success. **National Federation for Catholic Youth Ministry, 2001.** As parishes consider strategies to meet the needs of adolescent parishioners, they often consider the possibility of hiring a coordinator of youth ministry (CYM). How does a parish begin an effective hiring process? What does a competent CYM do? How can a parish find the right person? *Hiring for Youth Ministry* provides a step-by-step guide, practical tips, and reproducible handouts to assist in the hiring process.

Millennials Rising—The Next Great Generation. **Neil Howe and William Strauss. Vintage Books / Random House, 2000.** The phrase "kids these days" is infused with new meaning in this look at the generation born between 1982 and 2000. Arguing against the conventional wisdom that junior high and high school kids are disrespectful, violent, and alienated, Howe and Strauss demonstrate that the children of boomers and of older members of Generation X are actually hard workers and community builders.

Multicultural Religious Education. **Barbara Wilkerson, editor. Religious Education Press, 1997.** This book consists of a series of essays that discuss various aspects of multiculturalism in Christian religious education, as well as how the cultural influences of different racial groups impact their religious education.

National Certification Standards for Lay Ecclesial Ministers. **National Federation for Catholic Youth Ministry, 2000.** This resource provides a common vision for lay ministry formation, bringing clarity and definition to these pastoral roles. The document identifies five core standards, the common and specialized competencies, and codes of ethics for lay ecclesial ministers. A must-have for all ministerial leaders and those involved in ministry formation.

Passing On the Faith: A Radical New Model for Family and Youth Ministry. **Merton P. Strommen, PhD, and Richard A. Hardel, DMin. Saint Mary's Press, 2000.** What a radically new (yet ancient) model of faith formation: the family is restored to the center of the faith growth process, with the congregation and community as integral, active partners! The authors of this book present this new model, which is based on the extensive research of Search Institute and the Youth and Family Institute of Augsburg College, including the finding that only 10 percent of Church families (both Protestant and Catholic) discuss their faith on a regular basis.

Real Teens—A Contemporary Snapshot of Youth Culture. **George Barna. Regal Books, 2001.** They are the digital generation, the Mosaics, a new wave of connected and decidedly upbeat young people who are anxious to make a positive difference in the world around them. Skepticism, once the hallmark of Generation X, is waning as the prevalent attitude among teens. As teens change, so must our way of teaching them and reaching them. How can we effectively convey the eternal truths of the Gospels to high-tech, information-drenched, highly mobile youth who believe themselves to be self-sufficient? What are the challenges we face in reaching out to the Mosaic generation? And what are the opportunities they present? Once again, George Barna points the way.

Sometimes We Dance, Sometimes We Wrestle—Embracing the Spiritual Growth of Adolescents. **Michael Carotta. Harcourt Religion Publishers, 2002.** This resource blends research and real-life stories to describe four ways teachers, administrators, ministers, parents, coaches, and other adults can intentionally participate in the spiritual growth of adolescents.

The Vision of Catholic Youth Ministry: Fundamentals, Theory, and Practice. **Bob McCarty, general editor. Saint Mary's Press, 2005.** This resource provides an overview of the theory and pastoral practice of comprehensive youth ministry, based on the 1997 document *Renewing the Vision: A Framework for Catholic Youth Ministry.* Further, this resource serves as a foundational text for college undergraduate and graduate courses in youth ministry, as well as for diocesan ministry formation programs. Available in May 2005.

Youth Ministry and Parents: Secrets for a Successful Partnership. **Leif Kehrwald. Saint Mary's Press, 2004.** Because parents are the primary evangelizers of young people, they must be integrally involved in any successful youth ministry program. This book paves the way for youth ministers to create successful partnerships with parents of the teens in their parish. It helps youth ministers understand parents of teens and gives youth program leaders concrete strategies for enlisting parental support, overcoming resistance, and using the parental support system to complement youth ministry programs. This book is a must-have for every parish where youth ministers and parents understand the benefits of working together.

Youth Ministry in Rural and Small Town Settings: A Planning Resource. **National Federation for Catholic Youth Ministry, 1998.** This manual offers insights, assessment tools, and strategies for effective ministry to youth in rural and small-town settings. Because rural towns and small towns can share characteristics but also be vastly different, the NFCYM created this resource to help youth ministers understand and respond to the unique circumstances of each setting.

Acknowledgments

The scriptural quotations contained herein are from the New Revised Standard Version of the Bible, Catholic Edition. Copyright © 1993 and 1989 by the Division of Christian Education of the National Council of the Churches of Christ in the United States of America. All rights reserved.

The quotations marked *Vision of Youth Ministry* on pages 12 and 115 are from *A Vision of Youth Ministry*, by the United States Conference of Catholic Bishop's Department of Education (Washington, DC: USCCB, Inc., 1986), pages 6, 7 and 7, respectively. Copyright © 1986 by the USCCB, Inc. All rights reserved.

The quotations and excerpts marked *Renewing the Vision* on pages 12, 13, 13, 16, 17, 17–18, 18, 19, 19, 19–20, 19, 20, 20, 22, and 23 are from *Renewing the Vision: A Framework for Catholic Youth Ministry*, by the United States Conference of Catholic Bishop's (USCCB's) Department of Education (Washington, DC: USCCB, Inc., 1997), pages 9, 11, 15, 24, 25, 26, 27, 36, 36–37, 38, 40, 42, 44, 13, and 20, respectively. Copyright © 1997 by the USCCB, Inc. All rights reserved. Used with permission. No part of this work may be reproduced or transmitted in any form without permission in writing from the publisher.

The quotations marked *Putting Children and Families First* on pages 18, 18–19, and 19 are from *Putting Children and Families First: A Challenge for Our Church, Nation, and World,* by the Domestic Social Policy, International Policy, and Marriage and Family Life Committees (Washington, DC: USCCB, 1991), pages 14, 29, and 34, respectively. Copyright © 1992, 2002 by the USCCB, Inc. All rights reserved.

The excerpts on pages 19 and 30 are from *The Challenge of Catholic Youth Evangelization: Called to Be Witnesses and Storytellers,* by the Youth Outreach and Evangelization Subcommittee of the National Federation for Catholic Youth Ministry (NFCYM) (Washington, DC: NFCYM, Inc., 1993), pages 7–8 and 7. Copyright © 1993 by the NFCYM, Inc.

The second excerpt on page 23 is from Pope John Paul II's World Day of Prayer for Vocations, number 2, at *www.vatican.va/holy_father/john _paul_ii/messages/vocations/documents/hf_jp-ii_mes_18101994_world-day-for -vocations_en.html,* accessed October 13, 2004.

The prayer on page 28 is from the *Sacramentary,* English translation prepared by the International Commission on English in the Liturgy (ICEL) (New York: Catholic Book Publishing Co., 1985), page 552. English translation copyright © 1973 by the ICEL, Inc. All rights reserved. Used with permission.

The quotations on pages 28, 29, 30, 33, 43, 45, 48, 49, 50, 50, and 51 are quoted or adapted from *Constitution on the Sacred Liturgy (Sacrosanctum Concilium, 1963)*, numbers 7, 14, 43, 36, 10, 37, 52, 118, 7, 123, and 26, respectively, at *www.vatican.va/archive/hist_councils/ii_vatican_council/documents/vat-ii_const_19631204_sacrosanctum-concilium_en.html,* accessed October 13, 2004.

The excerpt on page 29 and the quotation on page 35 are from *The Vocation and the Mission of the Lay Faithful in the Church and in the World (Christifideles Laici),* numbers 46 and 47, at *www.vatican.va/holy_father/john_paul_ii/apost_exhortations/documents/hf_jp-ii_exh_30121988_christifideles-laici_en.html,* accessed August 12, 2004.

The second quotation on page 30 is from *The Challenge of Adolescent Catechesis: Maturing in Faith,* by the National Federation For Catholic Youth Ministry (NFCYM), number 24. Copyright © 1986 by the NFCYM, Inc. All rights reserved.

The first quotation on page 32 and the quotation on page 39 are from *Directory for Masses with Children,* by the Congregation for Divine Worship, numbers 1 and 9, at *www.adoremus.org/DMC-73.html,* accessed October 13, 2004.

The quotations marked *General Catechetical Directory* on pages 32, 40, 43–44, 63, and 78 are quoted and or adapted from *General Catechetical Directory,* by the Sacred Congregation for the Clergy, numbers 82, 25, 5, 17, and 84, respectively, at *www.vatican.va/roman_curia/congregations/cclergy/documents/rc_con_cclergy_doc_11041971_gcat_en.html,* accessed October 13, 2004.

The quotation marked Dilecti Amici on page 35 is from *Dilecti Amici,* Pope John Paul II's apostolic letter to the youth of the world on the occasion of International Youth Year, number 15, at *www.vatican.va./holy_father/john_paul_ii/apost_letters/documents/hf_jp-ii_apl_31031985_dilecti-amici_en.html,* accessed October 13, 2004.

The words of Pope John Paul II on page 37 are from his "World Youth Day Prayer Vigil," in *Origins,* August 26, 1993, page 185.

The quotations and excerpts marked *Catechesis in Our Time* on pages 40, 62, 62, 63, 63, 63, 63–64, 64, 66, 95, and 95 are from *Catechesis in Our Time (Catechesi Tradendae),* numbers 23, 5, 19, 23, 24, 16, 20, 38, 40, and 72, respectively, at *www.vatican.va/holy_father/john_paul_ii/apost_exhortations/documents/hf_jp-ii_exh_16101979_catechesi-tradendae_en.html,* accessed October 13, 2004.

The quotation on page 46 is from an English/Spanish compendium of *The Hispanic Presence: Challenge and Commitment, National Pastoral Plan for Hispanic Ministry,* and *Prophetic Voices: The Document on the Process of the III Encuentro Nacional Hispano de Pastoral,* by the USCCB, Inc. (Washington, DC: USCCB, Inc. 1993), page 41. Copyright © 1995 by the USCCB, Inc.

The quotations marked *General Instruction of the Roman Missal* on pages 46 and 49 are adapted from *General Instruction of the Roman Missal: Liturgy Documentary Series 2,* by the USCCB (Washington, DC: USCCB, 2003), numbers 313 and 13. English translation copyright © 2002 by International Commission on English in the Liturgy, Inc. Copyright © 2003 by the USCCB, Inc.

The second quotation on page 46 is from the English translation of the *Catechism of the Catholic Church* for use in the United States of America, number 2558. Copyright © 1994 by the United States Catholic Conference, Inc.—Libreria Editrice Vaticana. Used with permission.

The quotation on page 54 and the excerpt on page 57 are from *Called and Gifted for the Third Millennium,* by the USCCB (Washington, DC: USCCB, 1995), pages 15 and 21. Copyright © 1995 by the USCCB, Inc.

The quotation on pages 55–56 is adapted from *Music in Catholic Worship,* by the Bishops' Committee on the Liturgy (Washington, DC: USCCB, 1972), page 1. Copyright © 1972 by the USCCB, Inc.

The quotations on pages 69, 72, 72, 72, 88, 91, and 95 are from *Sharing the Light of Faith: National Catechetical Directory for Catholics of the United States,* by the USCCB (Washington, DC: USCCB, 1979), numbers 228, 176d, 176d, 176d, 211, 213, 217, and 218. Copyright © 1979 by the USCCB's Department of Education. This document is also found at *www.catholicculture.org/docs/doc_view.cfm?recnum=5294,* accessed October 13, 2004.

The quotations and excerpts on pages 100, 111, 112, 113, 116, 118, 120, 128, 128, 130, 130, and 131 are from *Evangelii Nuntiandi,* numbers 17, 18, 22, 21, 26, 22, 23, 59, 63, 75, 71, and 72, respectively, at *www.vatican.va./holy_father/paul_vi/apost_exhortations/documents/hf_p-vi_exh _19751208_evangelii-nuntiandi_en.html,* accessed October 13, 2004.

The information on the schema describing various styles of faith on pages 107–108 is adapted from *Will Our Children Have Faith?,* revised and expanded edition, by John H. Westerhoff III (New York: Morehouse Group, 2000), pages 89–99. Copyright © 2000 by Morehouse Group. Used with permission.

The quotation on page 122 and the quotation on pages 122–123 are from "Economic Justice for All," by the USCCB, numbers 47 and 46 at *www.osjspm.org/cst/eja.htm,* accessed October 13, 2004.

To view copyright terms and conditions for Internet materials cited within, log on to the home pages for the referenced Web sites.

During this book's preparation, all citations, facts, figures, names, addresses, telephone numbers, Internet URLs, and other pieces of information cited within were verified for accuracy. The authors and Saint Mary's Press staff have made every attempt to reference current and valid sources, but we cannot guarantee the content of any source, and we are not responsible for any changes that may have occurred since our verification. If you find an error in, or have a question or concern about, any of the information or sources listed within, please contact Saint Mary's Press.